PORTUGUESE STUDIES

VOLUME 26 NUMBER 2
2010

Founding Editor
HELDER MACEDO

Editors
FRANCISCO BETHENCOURT
RICARDO SOARES DE OLIVEIRA
JULIET PERKINS
LÚCIA SÁ
DAVID TREECE
ABDOOLKARIM VAKIL

Editorial Assistant
RICHARD CORRELL

Production Editor
GRAHAM NELSON

MODERN HUMANITIES RESEARCH ASSOCIATION

PORTUGUESE STUDIES

A biannual multi-disciplinary journal devoted to research on the cultures, societies, and history of the Lusophone world

International Advisory Board

DAVID BROOKSHAW	MARIA MANUEL LISBOA
JOÃO DE PINA CABRAL	KENNETH MAXWELL
IVO JOSÉ DE CASTRO	PAULO DE MEDEIROS
THOMAS F. EARLE	LAURA DE MELLO E SOUZA
JOHN GLEDSON	MARIA IRENE RAMALHO
ANNA KLOBUCKA	SILVIANO SANTIAGO

Articles to be considered for publication may be on any subject within the field but should not exceed 7,500 words and should be written in English. The Editorial Assistant is willing to undertake translations of texts from Portuguese if required; there will be a charge for this service. Contributions should be submitted in a form ready for publication in English and sent as an email attachment to the Editorial Assistant at richard.correll@kcl.ac.uk. The text should conform precisely to the conventions of the *MHRA Style Guide*, 2nd edn, 2008 (978-0-947623-76-0), obtainable from www.style.mhra.org.uk, price £6, US $15, €10; an online version is also available from the same address. Quotations and references should be carefully checked. Any quotations in Portuguese must be accompanied by an English translation. *Portuguese Studies* regrets that it must charge contributors with the cost of corrections in proof which the Editors in their discretion think excessive. Copies of books for review should be sent to The Reviews Editor, *Portuguese Studies*, Department of Portuguese and Brazilian Studies, King's College London, Strand, London WC2R 2LS, UK.

Copies of *Portuguese Studies* may be ordered from Subscriptions Department, Maney Publishing, Suite 1C, Joseph's Well, Hanover Walk, Leeds LS3 1AB, UK; email mhra@maney.co.uk. The journal is also available to individual members of the Modern Humanities Research Association in return for a composite membership subscription payable in advance. Further information about the activities of the MHRA and individual membership can be obtained from the Honorary Secretary, Dr Barbara Burns, School of Modern Languages and Cultures, University of Glasgow, Glasgow G12 8RS, or from the website at www.mhra.org.uk.

Parts of this work may be reproduced as permitted under legal provisions for fair dealing (or fair use) for the purposes of research, private study, criticism, or review, or when a relevant collective licensing agreement is in place. All other reproduction requires the written permission of the copyright holder who may be contacted at rights@mhra.org.uk.

ISSN 0267-5315
ISBN 978-1-907322-19-8

© 2010 THE MODERN HUMANITIES RESEARCH ASSOCIATION

Portuguese Studies vol. 26 no. 2

CONTENTS

Preface	132
History Recycled: Contemporary Performances of Shakespeare's *Richard II* at Portuguese National Theatres FRANCESCA CLARE RAYNER	134
Images of Defeat: Early Fado Films and the Estado Novo's Notion of Progress MICHAEL COLVIN	149
The Aquatic Unconscious: Water Imagery in Eça de Queirós's *A Cidade e as Serras* ESTELA VIEIRA	168
Zola in Rio de Janeiro: The Production of Space in Aluísio Azevedo's *O Cortiço* LÚCIA SÁ	183
The Brazil of Sílvio Romero and Machado de Assis: History of a 'Polemic', or the Writer as Critic of the Critic ALBERTO SCHNEIDER	205
A New Account of the Lisbon Earthquake: Marginalia in Joaquim José Moreira de Mendonça's *Historia Universal dos Terremotos* MARK MOLESKY	232
Abstracts	249

Preface

This issue of *Portuguese Studies* represents the diversity and richness of approaches to the cultures of the Portuguese-speaking world. The articles deal with the different meanings of staging Shakespeare in contemporary Portuguese theatre, the interaction of Fado and cinema in the Portugal of the 1930s, the structural symbolism of water in Eça de Queirós's novel *A Cidade e as Serras*, the crucial role of space in Aluísio Azevedo's novel *O Cortiço*, the debate between Machado de Assis and Sílvio Romero, and unpublished notes of a eyewitness of the Lisbon Earthquake of 1755. They feature innovative and interdisciplinary approaches, include new sources and experiment with new methods.

Francesca Clare Rayner studies two contemporary performances of Shakespeare's *Richard II* at the Portuguese National Theatres, staged by Carlos Avilez and Nuno Cardoso, representatives of two distinct generations of directors. She challenges the dismissal of political and aesthetic significance in the Portuguese theatre in the 1990s, showing how these new performances, based on a respectful approach or a playful appropriation, opened new directions in visual language and political intervention. Heritage theatre and aesthetic formalism, in the case of Avilez, are not equated with political conservatism, while postmodern ludic resistance, as the case of Cardoso, serves the deconstruction of male power.

Michael Colvin shows how the first two talkies in Portugal, Leitão de Barros's *A Severa* and Cottinelli Telmo's *A Canção de Lisboa*, shot before the establishment of Salazar's National Propaganda Office, reveal two different approaches, neither of which matched the regime's future ideological requirements. The former film stages, with faulty technology, a late Romantic novel by Júlio Dantas in a social environment of prostitutes and aristocrats, while the latter introduces updated technology, but within an ironic display of popular culture absorbed by the middle class. Fado is the common denominator, but the use is divergent, traditionalist and satirical, and both films clash with the subsequent nationalist and modernist framework favoured by António Ferro, the first to assume responsibility for National Propaganda.

Estela Vieira analyses the use of the element of water in Eça de Queirós's *A Cidade e as Serras*. Inspired by the seminal work of the philosopher Hans Blumenberg, *Shipwreck with Spectator*, she demonstrates the prolific and structural presence of water in the narrative: the flood of Jacinto's residence in Paris following the failure of a sophisticated hot water system; the jamming of a lift at an important dinner party, leaving the fish dish stuck down a lift-shaft; the fatal fish dinner that killed Jacinto's grandfather; and the violent storm that flooded the old farm belonging to Jacinto's family, dragging him back to Portugal. The metaphor of shipwreck is also used upon Jacinto's return to Portugal, giving a twist to the conflict between modernity and tradition lived by the main character that could have been projected on the nation.

Lúcia Sá challenges the Marxist critique of naturalism through a new study of spatial relations in the Brazilian novel *O Cortiço*. Inspired by Henri Lefebvre, she contests the idea of a mechanical or Darwinian conception of characters as products of their environment, in this case the tenement, showing how Rita Bahiana, João Romão, Pombinha and Bertoleza are truly individual characters, producing their own space. She criticizes the view that they are characters without social significance, reduced to their physiological condition or pathological behaviour, supposedly determined by the evolutionist framework. Most important of all, she shows that Aluísio Azevedo had a political agenda, with a deep sense of social injustice and class exploitation, far from the conservatism attributed by the tradition of Brazilian literary criticism, from Sílvio Romero to Flora Süssekind.

Alberto Schneider reverses the traditional relationship between writer and critic to suggest that Machado de Assis's novels represented an implicit critique of the interpretative principles adopted by Sílvio Romero. He approaches the question by examining how the two authors positioned themselves in the public debate on Brazilian nationality. Sílvio Romero's evolutionist, scientist and nationalist approach, blended with the nuanced idea of white supremacy in a mixed race country, is in confrontation with the cosmopolitan stance of Machado de Assis, who used different European literary influences to build his own style. Schneider considers that Romero was not mistaken in his analysis of Machado de Assis: the former targeted the latter, whose work mostly opposed his own conception of cultural and political intervention for the progress of Brazil, while Assis promoted a radically different and self-conscious aesthetic approach through his writings.

Mark Molesky publishes and analyses the anonymous marginalia written on a copy of Joaquim José Moreira de Mendonça's *Historia universal dos terremotos* (1758) preserved at the New York Public Library. The apparent eyewitness to the earthquake used this medium to give his (or her) fragmented account. The power of the tsunami is given much more importance than in other writings, particularly in relation to the destruction of the Terreiro do Paço, the Jardim do Tabaco, the Rua Nova and probably the remains of Philip II's walls. The author also asserts that the subsequent fire lasted for more than one month, a little-known aspect only confirmed by the recently discovered letters of the papal nuncio in Lisbon, Filippo Acciaiuoli. This article may encourage other researchers to publish more of the extraordinary marginalia buried in so many old books.

THE EDITORS

History Recycled: Contemporary Performances of Shakespeare's *Richard II* at Portuguese National Theatres

FRANCESCA CLARE RAYNER

Cultural Politics at the Turn of the New Millennium

In his 2003 'Shakespeare and the Cold War', Dennis Kennedy compares Shakespearean performance in the post-war period with performances at the turn of the twenty-first century. He concludes that 'compared to the postwar period much Shakespearean performance is adrift, either unexamined in its purpose or relying on heritage appeal, in keeping with postmodernist or consumerist notions of cultural production'. He ends with the deliberately polemical statement: '(i)n Shakespeare performance the Cold War is definitely over, and the capitalists have won.'[1]

This view of *fin-de-siècle* cultural production as lacking a clear political direction is shared by many, including the Portuguese theatre critic Eugénia Vasques. In her retrospective discussion of Portuguese theatre in the 1990s, she is dismissive of its political and aesthetic significance. Categorizing the period as 'a neo-Brechtian decade', she describes it as a decade when:

> [...] o nervosismo do fim-de-século se oculta nas figuras de distorção grotesca, a identidade nos motivos da desconstrução e em que a referência e a citação, como materiais de intercâmbio e de conhecimento, deram lugar, estética e eticamente, a processos de apropriação 'selvagem' sem má consciência culturalista e muito menos preconceitos de profunda mediação criativa.[2]

> [*fin-de-siècle* nervousness is hidden in grotesquely distorted figures, identity in deconstructionist impulses, and during which reference and citation, as materials of exchange and knowledge, give place, aesthetically and ethically, to processes of 'frenzied' appropriation without any cultural guilty conscience and much less any preconceived notions of deep creative mediation.]

Underlying both these assessments of theatre at the turn of the millennium is

---

[1] Dennis Kennedy, 'Shakespeare and the Cold War', in *Four Hundred Years of Shakespeare in Europe*, ed. by A. Luis Pujante and Ton Hoenselaars (Newark: University of Delaware Press, 2003), pp. 163–79 (pp. 176–77).

[2] Eugénia Vasques, *9 Considerações em Torno do Teatro em Portugal nos Anos 90* (Lisbon: Instituto Português das Artes do Espectáculo, 1998), p. 8.

a view of political performance informed by the 1960s and 1970s. It is a view indebted to Brechtian and counter-cultural models of a theatre anchored in social and political realities whose aim is to dispel false consciousness in audiences, as a prelude to political action and a construction of the political in performance that can only cast contemporary performance as lacking. This ignores the fact that the 1990s in Portugal was a decade which democratized the performance of Shakespeare, with not only a far larger number of performances of the plays but a greater diversification of companies performing them. Moreover, it was also a decade when there was a significant reconfiguration of gender roles, particularly in the Shakespeares performed at the Teatro Nacional São João, in Porto.[3] Therefore, any simple dismissal of the politics of performance in the new millennium — and there is certainly much that can be dismissed in this way — must be nuanced by a recognition of the ways in which understandings of the political were themselves in transformation.

In this essay I will question Kennedy's dismissal of heritage and postmodern theatre through a focus on two contemporary performances of Shakespeare's *Richard II* at Portuguese national theatres, in 1995 and 2007.[4] I will argue that heritage theatre might have a more positive meaning in a theatrical context such as the Portuguese which does not have a consistent tradition of performing Shakespeare, and that any such performance invariably contains within it dominant and emergent understandings of Shakespeare and Shakespearean performance. Secondly, I will illustrate how Kennedy's uncritical identification of postmodernism with consumerism sidelines the ways in which postmodern theatre's recognition of its implication in the discourses it seeks to challenge can represent an oppositional stance. The 2007 performance of the play staged a politics of disaffection which de-legitimized masculine political authority although it did not propose strategies of resistance to it. As such, it forms part of the cultural politics of postmodernism outlined by Johannes Birringer which opens up 'a space of intervention in which we may no longer see the revolution expected by Brecht, but realize the necessity to historicize the postmodern myths that postpone it'.[5]

---

[3] For an extended discussion of the performance of Shakespeare in Portugal during the nineties, with a particular focus on questions of gender and sexuality, see Francesca Clare Rayner, *Caught in the Act: The Representation of Sexual Transgression in Three Portuguese Productions of Shakespeare* (Braga: Centro de Estudos Humanísticos da Universidade do Minho, 2005).

[4] The former production of *Richard II* was directed by Carlos Avilez and performed at the Teatro Nacional Dona Maria II, Lisbon, from the 7 April 1995. The more recent *Richard II* was directed by Nuno Cardoso and was a co-production between the Teatro Nacional Dona Maria II in Lisbon and the Teatro Carlos Alberto in Porto, sister theatre of the Teatro Nacional São João, also in Porto. It was first performed on 13 June 2007.

[5] Johannes Birringer, *Theatre, Theory, Postmodernism* (Bloomington: Indiana University Press, 1991), p. 153.

Comparison of these two performances also offers an opportunity to foreground important generational shifts in Portuguese performances of Shakespeare around the new millennium. The director of the 1995 performances, Carlos Avilez, was in his late fifties at the time and had constructed a successful career, notably as one of the founder members of the Teatro Experimental de Cascais in 1965, before becoming Artistic Director of the main national theatre, the Teatro Nacional Dona Maria II in Lisbon. On the other hand, the director of the 2007 performances, Nuno Cardoso, was in his late thirties, had been Artistic Director of the Auditório Carlos Alberto in Porto and has been establishing a reputation as one of the most interesting young directors on the Portuguese theatrical scene.[6] Avilez had already directed Shakespeare twice, while for Cardoso this was his first Shakespeare as a director. This generational shift brings with it significant transformations in terms of ways of working with the Shakespearean text and the actors. Cardoso works extensively through improvisation and makes more far-reaching changes and cuts to the text than Avilez, who tends to favour visual transpositions of the text to the stage. This reveals a parallel ideological shift from a more reverential approach to Shakespeare in the case of Avilez compared to Cardoso's more ludic appropriations of the dramatist.

Heritage Theatre and *Richard II* at the Teatro Nacional Dona Maria II (1995)

Although the notion of heritage is often invoked in conjunction with drama, it is in the area of cinema that the paradoxes of heritage performance have been analysed more extensively.[7] In her introduction to the *Sight and Sound* collection *Film/Literature/Heritage* (2001), for instance, Ginette Vincendeau traces the historical transition from costume drama to heritage cinema. Films of this genre, she notes, are 'shot with high budgets and production values by A-list directors and they use stars, polished lighting and camerawork, many changes of décor and extras, well-researched interior designs, and classical or classical-inspired music.'[8] She notes the cultural similarities of such performances with contemporary museum culture and themed events, and explores divergent

---

[6] Avilez had directed *Hamlet* in 1987 and *King Lear* in 1990 and had also acted in *Romeo and Juliet* in 1987. He was Artistic Director of the Teatro Nacional D. Maria II from 1993 to 2000. Cardoso played Iago in performances of *Othello* in 2007, but his reputation was built on excellent stagings of Wederkind's *Spring Awakening* and Büchner's *Woyzeck* in Porto. He went on to direct a widely acclaimed *Platonov* by Chekhov at the São João in 2008.

[7] Although he does not make use of the term 'heritage theatre', the work of W. B. Worthen does examine in some detail the heritage characteristics of contemporary productions of Shakespeare. See, for example, his chapter on performances at the reconstructed Globe theatre in his *Shakespeare and the Force of Modern Performance* (Cambridge: Cambridge University Press, 2003), pp. 79–116.

[8] *Film/Literature/Heritage: A Sight and Sound Reader*, ed. by Ginette Vincendeau (London: BFI Publications, 2001), p. xviii.

approaches to the politics of such performances. On the one hand, their unashamed nostalgia and uncritical celebration of the past mean the genre 'has been condemned as conservative aesthetically and ideologically, promoting an idealized view of the past, and turning its back on contemporary issues'.[9] On the other hand, she signals the importance of the films' concentration on visual and aural pleasures and their recasting of ethnicity and gender as strategies to democratize the literary canon for contemporary audiences. She concludes that heritage films 'emerge as a pervasive and popular mode of film-making, in tune with both a *fin-de-siècle* passion for "museum culture" and a postmodern recycling of an increasingly mixed literary repertoire.'[10]

I would argue that a parallel critical notion of heritage theatre might usefully be applied to the Dona Maria II performances of *Richard II* in 1995. The political contradictions that Vincendeau foregrounds in heritage cinema are certainly pertinent here, where large-scale productions and production values acted as a smokescreen for political conservatism. However, while there are certainly good reasons to critique the politics of heritage theatre, it is also true that when such performances take place in countries like Portugal, where the performance of Shakespeare has been sporadic rather than consistent, heritage theatre assumes a pedagogical function that is more significant than in countries where Shakespeare is performed more regularly.[11] Performances of this kind can thus play a vital role in introducing wider audiences to the plays of Shakespeare, previously only seen by a very small, elite audience. Performance of Shakespeare was inconsistent before the 1990s and played for quite select audiences.[12] Moreover, performances tended to obey local rather than national interests. In such a context, the 1995 performances of *Richard II* presented for the first time on a national stage, constituted an invaluable opportunity to introduce audiences in Portugal to a little-known Shakespeare play.

The Teatro Nacional Dona Maria II *Richard II* was the first major production under the new Artistic Director, Carlos Avilez, and represented an obvious attempt to use the cultural currency of Shakespeare to stage a super-production which would confer legitimacy on the new administration.[13] 1995 was also the

---

[9] Ibid. p. xix.
[10] Ibid. p. xxiv.
[11] The cultural insularity and censorship of the Portuguese dictatorship was largely responsible for the lack of a tradition of performance of Shakespeare's plays in Portugal from the very early 1930s up until the Revolution in 1974. Although the Salazar–Caetano dictatorship claimed to support the creation of a national culture and there were some performances of Shakespeare at the National Theatre during this period, Salazar's sense of a national culture was of an insular, folkloric Portuguese cultural heritage which confirmed moral and political orthodoxy. Performances of Shakespeare were seen as marginal to this process.
[12] For additional information on performances of Shakespeare in Portugal, consult the excellent *Centro de Estudos de Teatro* database at <http://www.fl.ul.pt/CETbase/default.htm> [accessed 17 March 2010].
[13] Signs of the performances' super-production pretensions can be seen in the use of 'star actors', the fact that a total of sixty-two people were involved in the production, the huge

year in which national elections brought António Guterres to power as Prime Minister, as he defeated Aníbal Cavaco Silva at the polls. These political events, according to the actor Luís Assis, who played Percy in the performances, impacted on Avilez's thinking about the play.[14] Assis recounts that when Avilez first spoke to the cast, he reinforced the topicality of the play by referring to the current political context. Reading between the lines, Assis felt this meant that Avilez saw the deposed Cavaco Silva as a sort of Richard II figure, deposed as a despot by the usurper Bullingbrook (read Guterres), who would then go on to become an even worse despot in the course of time. However, in a comment to the journalist Catarina Carvalho, Avilez himself preferred to stress the play's parallels with recent political corruption scandals.[15]

The performances were strongly characterized by aesthetic formalism. The magnificent scenography and elaborate costumes evoked the ceremony and ritual of a medieval court in all its splendour, with the lonely, mercurial figure of Richard (Carlos Daniel) at its centre. It is worth singling out in this respect the stunning but sparse set design by José Manuel Castanheira, an internationally recognized scenographer who had worked previously with Avilez on his *King Lear*, created around doors, bridges and elevatory mechanisms. A series of vivid onstage panels by the painter Graça Morais likened the gradual encirclement of Richard to a hunt where Richard was cast as a stag. A musical score was especially composed by the jazz composer António Pinho Vargas, based on the music of Handel and on French opera, reinforcing the ceremonial aspect of the performances towards the beginning, and Richard's solitude later on. Costume design was meticulously researched in the National Portrait Gallery in London, once more by Graça Morais.

However, while these aspects of the staging made excellent use of some of the best contemporary practitioners in the arts, the background material published to accompany the performances consigned the political questions raised by the play to those of medieval England, notably the question of the divine right of kings and the limited scope within which subjects could legitimately rebel.[16] The critical texts included in this material conveyed a sense of the history informing the play as consensual and orderly, and of the play as a great work of literature rather than a text written for performance. Apart from articles by Stanley Wells

---

budget for the performances, and the fact that the performances lasted initially for a total of four hours with two intervals being added at a later stage. Critical reviews also reinforced its status as a super-production with descriptions of it as magnificent, luxurious, stunning and monumental. The amount of money spent on the performances was a matter of concern to some journalists, such as Carlos Porto, but even he was able to excuse this on the grounds of the rarity of such an event on the Portuguese stage. *Jornal de Letras*, 28 April 1995, p. 31.

[14] Personal email communication from the actor. My thanks to Luís Assis for this suggestion.

[15] Avilez commented that the play 'nos faz lembrar escândalos políticos recentes' [reminds us of recent political scandals] in an article by Catarina Carvalho, 'Ricardo segundo Avilez' in *Diário de Notícias*, 8 April 1995, p. 29.

[16] *William Shakespeare, Ricardo II: Textos de Apoio*, Teatro Nacional Dona Maria II, 1995.

and Fernando de Mello Moser, the material all preceded the 1980s. The longest extract, from E. M. W. Tillyard's *Shakespeare's History Plays*, was published in 1944.[17] This is not to suggest these works did not continue to have their value, but it is telling that criticism from the 1980s onwards, particularly the work of the English cultural materialists and American new historicists, which is much more political in its approach, was absent from the thinking behind the play. It suggests not only a certain cultural insularity of the theatre, but also an unwillingness to politicize Shakespeare in such a way that his status — and therefore the theatre's status in performing him — might be undermined.

However, in the overwhelmingly positive newspaper reviews of the performances, parallels were indeed drawn between the politics of the play and those of present day Portugal.[18] Tito Lívio's review in *A Capital*, for instance, noted the highlighting of contemporary political questions such as 'a perversão do poder e o clientelismo político' [the perversion of power and political clientelism].[19] Manuel João Gomes, in his article in the newspaper *Público* entitled 'Trabalho de Shakespeare no Dona Maria' remarked that '(a)pesar de vivermos em regime republicano e democrático, o perigo de identificação não está posto de lado' [although we live in a Republican, democratic regime, this does not prevent audiences identifying with the regime on-stage].[20] This may have represented a reading of the play rather than the performances, but it illustrates that this first production of the play in Portugal on a national stage could be appropriated to debate present-day questions pertaining to the sphere of national politics.

More significantly, even if the dominant perspective in this example of

[17] E. M. W. Tillyard, *Shakespeare's History Plays* (London: Chatto & Windus, 1944).
[18] The only negative review I have come across is one in *Visão*, 11 May 1995, p. 98, by Rosário Anselmo, who complains that the production would have benefited if Avilez had put more emphasis on conceptual rigour than what she labels 'uma sobrevalorização formal' [a formal over-valorization]. She also criticizes the 'disparidade de estilos e leituras' [disparity of styles and readings] among the actors and, like several other critics, singles out the weak acting of Fernando Luís as Bullingbrook against Carlos Daniel's skilful Richard.
[19] Tito Lívio, review in *A Capital*, 4 May 1995, p. 54. In another review in *A Capital*, 8 April 1995, p. 20, under the title 'Ricardo II leva esplendor cenográfico ao Nacional: Carlos Avilez encena Shakespeare político' [Richard II brings scenographic splendour to the National Theatre: Carlos Avilez stages a political Shakespeare], Rita Bertrand quotes the actor who played Bushy, Ricardo Carriço, as saying about his character: 'É um deslumbrado, obcecado pelo poder e oportunista. Há muita gente como ele na nossa sociedade' [He is dazzled, obsessed by power and an opportunist. There are many people like him in our society].
[20] The quotation in the text from Manuel João Gomes is taken from his article 'Trabalho de Shakespeare no Dona Maria' in *Público*, 7 April 1995, *Zoom*, pp. 1–5 (p. 2). Many reviewers couched their political comments within a universalizing discourse. For example, João Carneiro's review entitled 'A noite luminosa', in *Expresso*, 14 April 1995, *Revista*, p. 123, noted that 'O poder é sempre motor de um desejo irrepressível, conseguido e mantido pela violência, pela traição e pelo assassínio' [power always drives an irrepressible desire, achieved and maintained through violence, treachery and murder].

heritage theatre relied on an excessive aesthetic formalism to distance the politics of the play, other emergent perspectives can be glimpsed on the margins of the performances. As the theatre's resident company had not undergone renewal for many years, the performances made use of the remit of the 'artista convidada' [invited performer], to counter the theatre's long-term deficiencies by using artists outside the company structure for the production run. The painter Graça Morais and the choreographer Olga Roriz were both involved in the production on just such a one-off basis, as was the television and cinema actor, Fernando Luís, who played Bullingbrook. The translator and dramaturg Maria João da Rocha Afonso was also responsible for a new translation of the play. As such, although the integration of these artists enabled the Dona Maria in the short-term to claim a theatrical health it didn't in fact possess, in the long-term, tendencies such as the greater involvement of women in Shakespearean productions, the prominence of freelancers, the nod to other media like the visual arts, television and cinema and the recourse to academics as translators and dramaturgs, all of which became so central in the theatre work of the late 1990s, suggest new directions in the performance of Shakespeare which were to question the dominant premises of text-based heritage theatre through a renewed interest in the visual and aural languages of the stage. In Maria João da Rocha Afonso's contribution to the production programme, there is even a hint that future studies of Shakespeare should give equal status to both performance and text, and in her introduction, she argues that 'a análise académica serve o palco, o palco enriquece o trabalho de aula' [academic analysis serves the stage, and the stage enriches classroom work].[21] Moreover, it is noticeable that in comparison with the claims for the universality of a stable text, the brief section on performance of the plays in the background material is explicitly contingent, noting the ways in which interpretations of the play in performance have changed significantly over the years.[22] In this sense, performance of Shakespeare is functioning as a 'school' where theatre practitioners can develop new ideas about Shakespearean performance, even within an apparently unchallenging set of performative circumstances.

Yet perhaps the most curious sign of things to come in these performances was a strongly homoerotic nude bathing scene between Richard (Carlos Daniel) and Aumerle (José Neves). Although its significance was little discussed in the reviews, nudity was certainly rare on the stage of the Teatro Nacional and homoeroticism was invariably played down.[23] This might then seem somewhat

---

[21] Maria João da Rocha Afonso, Production programme, p. 7 ('Um desafio').

[22] *Textos de Apoio*, p. 16 ('*Ricardo II* no Teatro'). Although the authors of the individual texts, edited by Maria João da Rocha Afonso, are not identified, this particular piece appears to draw on the Cambridge School Shakespeare edition of *Richard II*, ed. by Michael Clamp (Cambridge: Cambridge University Press, 1992).

[23] Carlos Porto in his article in the *Jornal de Letras* (see note 13) thought the episode 'desnecessário' [unnecessary] while Eugénia Vasques, in *Expresso*, 29 April 1995, *Cartaz*, p. 13, merely hinted at homosexuality as a possible reason for Richard's downfall.

out of place in a production characterized by political conservatism, but it should be seen within the production's general emphasis on visual splendour and, as such, represented little more than a slightly piquant moment in a predominantly safe production. While on the one hand this scene harked back to Avilez's early reputation as an *enfant terrible* with a predilection for performing Genet, it also looked forward to more overt and diversified representations of dissident forms of sexuality towards the end of the millennium.[24]

The Politics of Postmodern Performance: *Richard II* at the Teatro Nacional Dona Maria II and the Teatro Carlos Alberto (2007)

In contrast to the earlier Dona Maria performances, the 2007 co-production of the play at the Dona Maria II and the Teatro Carlos Alberto in Porto was strongly focused on the present and made use of a variety of postmodern techniques. In one of the few theoretical discussions of the politics of postmodern performance, Philip Auslander argues in his chapter 'Towards a Concept of the Political in Postmodern Theatre' that while postmodernism 'has not rendered political theatre impossible [...] it has made it necessary to rethink the whole project of political art'.[25] He details the ways in which postmodernism has prompted a shift from 'transgressive to resistant political art', in other words, from a belief that it is possible to critique existing power structures from a position outside of them, as in the Brechtian political project, to a post-structuralist acknowledgement that political contestation is inevitably bound up in the discourses it seeks to challenge. Central to Auslander's argument for the political efficacy of postmodern theatre is what he labels its 'critique of presence'. This critique stems from a recognition that the presence, or what we might call the charisma, attributed to certain performers by their audiences is intimately tied in with the repetition of forms of illusionist theatre that uphold existing power structures in their claim to show things 'as they are' in 'real life'. Charisma discourages the critical distance necessary to question that power by charming or frightening the audience into submission. A critique of presence therefore implies putting on show the mechanisms which construct charismatic presence, through what Auslander labels the performer's 'disinvestment of

---

[24] Performances at the Teatro Nacional São João, such as their 1998 *Noite de Reis*, are examples of this trend. Cf. Francesca Clare Rayner, *Caught in the Act*.
[25] Philip Auslander, *From Acting to Performance: Essays in Modernism and Postmodernism* (London and New York: Routledge, 1997), p. 58. The only book-length study of theatre and postmodernism I have come across is the work by Johannes Birringer. In the Portuguese context, Ana Gabriela Macedo's recently published analysis of postmodernism specifically focuses upon questions of gender: *Narrando o pós-moderno: Reescritas, re-visões, adaptações*, (Braga: Centro de Estudos Humanísticos da Universidade do Minho, 2008); while Paulo Eduardo Carvalho's biography of Ricardo Pais explores in detail Pais's use of postmodern techniques in the performances he directs: *Ricardo Pais: Actos e Variedades* (Porto: Campo das Letras, 2006).

self'.²⁶ In this way, the charismatic performance is deconstructed to reveal the unstable basis of both theatrical and political power.

What is striking about this contemporary understanding of postmodern political performance is how small a distance separates representation from a critique of representation, for performers must first place themselves in charismatic roles in order to deconstruct them. This means that it is often difficult to establish whether political interventions in postmodern performance point effectively towards alternatives or simply re-establish the status quo in a slightly modified form. Indeed, Auslander argues that such contradictions are inherent to his project of a resistant, postmodern, political performance practice as they illustrate how 'if we're to position ourselves politically, we must be prepared to contend with the commodification of politics which levels discourses and masks difference, and the mediatization by which the dominant ideology nullifies the counterhegemonic'.²⁷

In the specific domain of gender, Auslander notes how performance's association of the textual with male performers and the visual with female performers 'occupies another uncomfortable space, neither clearly sexist nor clearly deconstructing', although this does not lead to further discussion of ways in which gender inflects notions of charismatic presence.²⁸ Yet, we need only consider the mediatized candidacies of Hillary Clinton and Barack Obama to understand the differential processes which construct distinct visions of charismatic men and women. One of the features of the 2007 *Richard II* that most interested me, therefore, was the ways in which its postmodern parody of presence was aimed at the obviously gendered bodies of male authority figures, thus disinvesting patriarchal power of its textual and political authority, whilst also enabling women performers temporarily to occupy these redefined spaces of male presence.

The critique of masculine presence

I would like to begin my discussion of the second performance of *Richard II* by examining a group photograph of the male performers (Fig. 1).²⁹ With their ill-fitting clothes, they resemble a group of men meeting for a Sunday morning football match rather than the elite set of nobles who are to decide the destiny of a feudal English kingdom. Indeed the innovative set design by Fernando Ribeiro, who had worked with Cardoso on previous productions, was a representation of a football pitch complete with floodlights, a particularly fluid stage setting for the play.³⁰ The central figure, the actor João Ricardo

---

²⁶ Auslander, p. 67.
²⁷ Ibid, p. 70.
²⁸ Ibid, p. 65.
²⁹ My thanks to the Teatro Nacional São João and its archivist Paula Braga for providing me with these production photographs. The photographer is Margarida Dias.
³⁰ A reading of the performances as reinforcing parallels between the political sphere and

Production shots, taken in Lisbon, from Shakespeare's *Richard II*, performed at the Teatro Carlos Alberto, Porto, and the Teatro Nacional Dona Maria II, Lisbon, Portugal, in 2007. Photographs taken by Margarida Dias. Reproduced by courtesy of the archive service of the Teatro Nacional São João, Porto.
FIG. 1 (above): Central figure King Richard II, played by João Ricardo.
FIG. 2 (below): Foreground figure Bullingbrook, played by Gonçalo Amaral.

as Richard II, has obviously been drinking to excess, judging by the size of his stomach, and cannot hope to command respect from others in a pair of unflattering shorts with his socks around his ankles. While the actor playing Richard II is traditionally thin and rather effeminate, this corpulent, sweaty, very masculine performer signals his difference. Similarly, instead of the conventional ceremonial and highly stylized encounters between the characters in this play about medieval history, these male performers stormed round the stage at high speed, occasionally coming together in homoerotically charged groupings reminiscent of televised encounters between football teams.

By way of contrast (Fig. 2), we have the dangerously thin actor playing Bullingbrook (Gonçalo Amaral). The contrast between the fat Richard and the thin Bullingbrook evokes a series of volatile signifiers between fat, lack of control and self-indulgence on the one hand and thinness, self-denial, untrustworthiness and lack of sociability on the other. Neither appears to merit our confidence. Although the male characters behind Bullingbrook (and if you look carefully to the right of the picture you can see that some of them are played by actresses) continue to run round the makeshift football pitch under the glare of the floodlight, Bullingbrook himself seems decontextualized and uninterested in those desperately seeking the non-existent ball. The discarded shirts on the ground indicate that the team members have changed sides and changed leaders, but this seems to have made very little difference.

In what ways do such representations of masculine authority enact political interventions? In an interview published just before the opening performances, the director Nuno Cardoso suggested reasons why the politics of the play felt contemporary to him:

> A peça interessa-me porque reflecte sobre uma dupla condição do indivíduo: o homem privado e o homem público, investido de poder. Depois, é um texto onde os mecanismos do poder são centrais: no núcleo da história há uma transferência de poder, que não é uma sucessão, mais uma deposição. E nos dias de hoje, o poder, a maneira como as pessoas o exercem e a forma como reagem aqueles sobre quem ele é exercido, é uma questão sobre a qual me parece que não reflectimos suficiente, em democracia.[31]

---

the cultural in terms of the importance attributed to football in Portugal within the wider culture lies beyond the scope of this article, but would be an interesting topic for further research.

[31] Unascribed article entitled 'Gosto de risco e arrisco constantantemente' in the Teatro Nacional Dona Maria II magazine *Jornal de Teatro*, 11 May 2007, p. 4. In an interview included in the production programme entitled 'O teatro é uma das artes em que a carnalidade é mais imediata', Cardoso hints at the way in which notions of politics and the politician had changed from the 1980s onwards: 'Em conversa com os actores, falávamos de uma certa forma de fazer política que descende das grandes esperanças do pós-25 de Abril e que de repente deu lugar ao aparecimento de um político mais tecnocrata, mais seco. Isso fez-se sentir em Portugal no final dos anos 80, início dos 90, e de certa forma permanece até hoje' [In conversation with the actors, we spoke about a certain way of doing politics which comes from the great expectations of the post-25 April period, and which suddenly gave

[The play interests me because it reflects on the dual condition of the individual: the private man and the public man, invested with power. And then, it is a text where the mechanisms of power are central: at the core of the narrative there is a transfer of power, which is not a succession but a deposal. And in our own time, power, the way that people exercise it and the way in which those over whom it is exercised react, is a matter on which it seems to me that we do not reflect sufficiently, in our democracy.]

This dual interest, not only in those who exercise power but also in those over whom it is exercised, indicates the ways in which the performance's parodic critique of charismatic male authority functioned politically. For if charisma is projected onto an authority figure by an audience of subjects who thus confirm their subjection, the deconstruction of presence disavows such projections and encourages what Vera Frenkel has characterized as 'a non-charismatic understanding which permits us not to believe so readily in the other as the keeper of our treasure and our disease'.[32] As such, if political leaders only have power because their subjects make them powerful, then to have both Richard and Bullingbrook performed so uncharismatically makes the basis of their power appear not only unstable but, crucially, transformable.

The politics of gender and genre in performance

As Jean E. Howard and Phyllis Rackin point out, in the second tetralogy of Shakespearean history plays which begins with *Richard II*, 'women's roles are further constricted. There are fewer female characters, they have less time on stage and less to say when they get there.'[33] Contemporary performance can merely confirm women's textual absence or highlight the differences between the historical past and the contemporary present through rethinking performances strategies for women. This performance of *Richard II* was very much an ensemble creation and although specific roles such as the Queen, the Duchess of Gloucester and the Duchess of York were played by women performers, and the majority of male roles were played by male performers, the sparseness of the female roles was compensated for to a certain extent by

---

way to the appearance of a more technocratic, more arid politician. This made itself felt in Portugal in the late 1980s and early 1990s, and in a way persists until today] (p. 22). Cardoso also notes the responsibility of this generation of politicians in encouraging political apathy: 'Actualmente é comum alegar-se o desinteresse do cidadão em relação à política. Mas a forma como a política se exerce é de molde a deixar o cidadão completamente de fora' [At the moment a disengagement by the citizen towards politics is commonly alleged. But the way that politics is conducted is of a kind that leaves the citizen completely on the outside] (p. 23). Production programme for TNDM/TNSJ *Ricardo II*, Teatro Nacional Dona Maria II, 2007.

[32] *apud* Auslander, p. 63.
[33] Jean E. Howard and Phyllis Rackin, 'Richard II', in *Engendering a Nation: A Feminist Account of Shakespeare's English Histories* (London and New York: Routledge, 1997), pp. 137–59 (p. 137).

the actress who played the Duchess of Gloucester (Flávia Gusmão) doubling as the jailer, and the actress who played the Duchess of York (Marta Gorgulho) doubling as the noble Willoughby. These were minor roles, but such regendering or cross-gender casting has been rare in Portuguese theatre and thus represents a small but significant step towards ensuring theatrical equality for actors and actresses in the performance of Shakespeare — especially since the three actresses also took their places alongside the actors during the many ensemble scenes. Such moves further deconstructed connections between masculinity and theatrical and political authority by extending the performance of masculinity to women performers, although the irony of enabling women to occupy masculine subject positions only when they have been de-legitimized remains politically ambiguous. Perhaps the most visible sign of this ambiguity for women in the performances was their stage costumes. Cardoso worked with the radically inventive fashion design team 'Storytailors' to create outrageous, eclectic costumes for the woman characters which could not be related to any specific historical period. Yet however visually striking these costumes, it is also true that they were far more difficult to move about in and far more physically constricting than the costumes for the male characters.

The entrance of the Duchess of York towards the end of *Richard II* is usually credited with the eruption of domestic farce into the nobler genre of historical tragedy.[34] Her embarrassing knelt appeal to Bullingbrook to save her son from execution irritates both Bullingbrook and the Duke of York as an unwelcome familial intervention in affairs of state. Yet in this performance, farce undermined historical tragedy throughout the play. The dominant political metaphor of the performances was the persistent transfer of the crown. At regular intervals, burlesque music started up an anarchic stage game where the crown was passed between actors and actresses in a circle until the music stopped. Through this wonderfully carnivalesque staging of the circularity of power, such sequences subverted the genre of historical tragedy by recasting transfers of power as farce, where characters spun round on what Nicoleta Cimpoes has called, 'the dizzy merry-go-round of history'.[35] Moreover, Richard's emotional final speeches in prison were spoken by the actor face-down on the stage, deconstructing the intense pathos of these speeches through an apparent inability to communicate them.[36] At the end of the performance

---

[34] Howard and Rackin note the way in which the episode with the Duchess of York 'lowers the tone to domestic comedy', *Engendering a Nation*, p. 56. Leonard Barkan has also remarked on the textual elements of farce, bathos and 'semi-comic dramaturgy' that distinguish Bullingbrook's rule from Richard's in 'The Theatrical Consistency of *Richard II*', *Shakespeare Quarterly*, 29 (1975), pp. 5–19 (p. 17). These performances, however, suggested such elements were as present during Richard's reign as they are in Bullingbrook's.

[35] Nicoleta Cimpoes, 'Theatrics at War: When *Macbeth* Meets *Macbett*', unpublished paper presented at the 2007 Shakespeare in Europe Conference, in a seminar entitled 'Performance after 1989/90', University of Iasi, Romania (p. 9).

[36] I am assuming that this was intentional on the part of the actor and director and not just

(v. 6), the characters were paired together in a dance which extended the notion of the circularity of power beyond the text.[37] The final couple were Bullingbrook and Richard who waltzed their way to the front of the stage where Richard stole Bullingbrook's crown in performative revenge for his textual usurpation.

Following the dance, this sense of power as farce keyed into the cynical contemporary mediatization of politics. When Bullingbrook addressed his plea for forgiveness for Richard's coming murder to the audience rather than to the assembled cast around him (v. 6. 38–52), the plea was framed as just another example of political spin by an adroit, media-friendly new ruler. In a country like Portugal where the Socialist government, and in particular its leader, José Sócrates, is known to be acutely sensitive about its public image in the media, such an appropriation of the play represented a highly pertinent political intervention.

Yet if the performance de-legitimized contemporary male political authority through parody, what did it put in its place? Is there not a risk — to return to one of the most frequent critiques of postmodernism — that it merely aestheticizes political impotence in its suggestion that fundamentally all forms of politics and politicians are alike? Johannes Birringer has spoken of 'the tenacious memory that the theatre can have of the history of dispossession'.[38] Such micro-narratives of dispossession highlight the increasingly unequal political relationship between the powerful and the powerless. In this *Richard II*, ten or more suitcases were packed and repacked onstage at regular intervals as the soldiers of the two armies trooped wearily from place to place, a potent visual reminder of the consequences for the wider population of power struggles among elites. This also seemed an apt metaphor for the Portuguese theatrical performer in the current globalized marketplace, selling his or her intercultural wares out of a standardized suitcase to an audience which is, in the words of Herbert Blau, '*declassified*' and whose power as an audience 'is not the spontaneously live ideology but the fringe benefit of collective dispossession'.[39]

The current international financial and environmental crises are revealing the contradictions of late capitalism more starkly than theatre ever could.

---

a case of bad acting. In general, however, the disturbingly sinister performance of Gonçalo Amaral as Bullingbrook was vastly more subtle and effective than that of João Ricardo as Richard, perhaps emblematic of yet another generational shift in terms of acting skills.

[37] The edition of *Richard II* used throughout is the New Cambridge Shakespeare, ed. by Andrew Gurr (Cambridge: Cambridge University Press, 2003).

[38] Johannes Birringer, p.166.

[39] Herbert Blau, *The Audience* (Baltimore, MD: Johns Hopkins University Press, 1990), p. 357. Nuno Cardoso simultaneously worked on another performance of the play, *R2*, with the young people in the underprivileged Lisbon neighbourhood of Cova da Moura, explicitly indicating his concern with the contemporary dispossessed. Here the figure of Richard II became the *Presidente da Junta de Freguesia*.

Indeed, theatre is not immune to such processes as seen by the transformation of the Dona Maria II into a public limited company in the new millennium. Their 1995 performance of *Richard II* appears to endorse the negative views of the politics of performance suggested by Dennis Kennedy and Eugénia Vasques, particularly Kennedy's view of performance during this period as 'adrift' and 'unexamined in its purpose', yet this would be to ignore the ways in which the performances were used by theatrical and artistic practitioners to create new autonomous spaces for the visual and aural languages of performance. The 2007 co-production of *Richard II*, on the other hand, suggests the emergence of a reconfigured notion of the political in the new millennium. What is intriguing about postmodern theatre work in the contemporary context is that its later appearance in Portuguese theatre coincides with its critique; in other words, as it begins to become visible, it also suggests what it might lack. In this particular instance, recognition that postmodern work has often ignored questions of gender coincided with concrete steps to foreground this through postmodern strategies which in turn pointed to the need to situate performance socially and historically. Such a multi-directional approach to the political may lack the certainties of the political theatre work of a Brecht or of an Augusto Boal. Nevertheless, it is a form of political theatre work in national theatres which is, in the words of Dan Rebellato 'appropriate for an age in which the national political institutions are being overpowered by global capital, and the international institutions that might give contingent force to our developing cosmopolitan sense have not yet been built.'[40]

UNIVERSIDADE DO MINHO

---

[40] Dan Rebellato, 'From the State of the Nation to Globalization: Shifting Political Agendas in Contemporary British Playwriting', in *A Concise Companion to British and Irish Drama*, ed. by Nadine Holdsworth and Mary Luckhurst (Malden, MA, Oxford, and Victoria: Blackwell, 2008), pp. 245–62 (p. 259).

Images of Defeat: Early Fado Films and the Estado Novo's Notion of Progress

MICHAEL COLVIN

In 1931, when Portugal can finally see and hear herself in sound movies, that most progressive of contemporary visual art forms, her incarnation is Maria Severa, 'the gypsy harlot [with whom] a little bit of Portugal's soul died.'[1] The fact that Leitão de Barros's Franco-Portuguese production of *A Severa* — Júlio Dantas's story of a pathetic nineteenth-century prostitute whose untouchable social class combined with her surrender to fate is the source of all of her suffering — should be Portugal's first talkie indicates the Estado Novo's uphill battle to penetrate the national psyche with its obsessive modernizing aesthetics.[2] Two years later, Cottinelli Telmo's irreverent *A Canção de Lisboa* announces itself as Portugal's first talkie, and we are left wondering why, in light of the Estado Novo's anti-fado rhetoric, a second *fadista* film should mark the birth of the young regime's ideological progress. Whereas *Severa* and *Canção* appear before the establishment of Portugal's ministry of propaganda, these films do not adhere to the regime's prescription for national cinema. As a result, these privileged movies present values and images that, shortly thereafter, will be purged from Portuguese cinema for the rest of the decade: values linked to a people who are dissatisfied with the previous quarter of a century of experimental democracy, yet who are cynical about the seemingly progressive ideals of the nascent State. And as the Fado, bullfights, and folklore are common motifs in *Severa* and *Canção*, these films allow us to observe a dialogue between Portugal's first talkies and to catch a glimpse of the Nation's popular culture before the Estado Novo's propaganda has a chance to recontextualize it to promote its own agenda.

After two decades of political turmoil following the fall of the monarchy (1910), and the coup d'état of the First Republic (1926), the Estado Novo would dig its heels into popular culture through carefully planned propaganda. In an early conversation, the future Minister of National Propaganda, António

---

[1] Júlio Dantas, *A Severa* (Porto: Porto Editora, 1994), p. 236. I thank my friend, Hugo Lobo de Sousa for having lent me his DVD copy of Leitão de Barros's *A Severa*.

[2] João Bénard da Costa, *Histórias do Cinema* (Lisbon: Imprensa Nacional–Casa da Moeda, 1991), p. 52; M. Felix Ribeiro, *Filmes, Figuras e Factos da História do Cinema Português, 1896–1949* (Lisbon: Cinemateca Portuguesa, 1983), pp. 281–82, José Leitão de Barros filmed *A Severa*'s outdoor scenes in Portugal. He shot the indoor scenes, and added sound to the outdoor scenes, at the Tobis Studios in Paris.

Ferro — then a young journalist who had just returned from an interview with Mussolini — proposed to Salazar the political value of the contemporary arts, following the model of Italian fascism: 'If it is just and necessary to think about the preservation of our artistic heritage, it is equally just, and perhaps more urgent to think about the living arts that should accompany our evolution, that should be the expression of our era.'[3] The business of creating Portugal's artistic showpiece would be a sombre one, because, as Bénard da Costa explains, the Estado Novo did not want to be remembered on screen for a few jokes: 'What mattered was breathing life into [eight centuries] of history [...] or exalting the grandeur of the present.'[4]

And herein lies the great aesthetic contradiction of the Secretariado da Propaganda Nacional (SPN) that would mark Portuguese artistic production for some decades: the reconciliation of a glorious past with a promising future; the struggle between tradition and progress; the incongruity of pre-Republican tastes alongside a twentieth-century fascistic aesthetics. In Portugal, the nineteenth century's cultural end was near. And as far as Ferro was concerned, the Estado Novo would be a breath of fresh air in a decaying society that was clinging to tardo-Romantic ideals. Therefore, naturally, in 1933, the young regime was fed up with *revistas* [musical reviews], Fados and *cegadas* [vaudevillian drag shows], the dominant forms of entertainment for early twentieth-century urban Portuguese society.[5] So, when Chianca de Garcia, on the heels of Cottinelli's success, proposed as Portugal's third talkie a musical comedy in the vein of *Canção*, he was told that the Nation was ready for something nobler, more austere.[6]

---

[3] Artur Portela, *Salazarismo e Artes Plásticas* (Lisbon: Instituto de Cultura e Língua Portuguesa, 1982), p. 18; António Ferro, *Salazar* (Lisbon: Empresa Nacional de Publicidade, 1933), p. 89. Bénard da Costa, p. 43 n. 32, mentions that Ferro's critics referred to him as the 'Portuguese Goebbels'. Ibid., pp. 36–37, clarifies that we can only compare Portuguese Salazarism with Italian Fascism and German Nazism in terms of the effects of the regimes' propaganda. He adds that although Ferro's promotion of the 'política do espírito' [politics of the soul] proposed a monolithic Portuguese cultural identity with the goals of controlling the masses through native folklore, the Minister of National Propaganda was a Modernist, and thus seduced by the avant garde, much to the chagrin of Salazar, the conservatives and national folklore.

[4] Ibid., p. 55.

[5] Ibid., p. 55, remarks that *A Severa* and *A Canção* subscribe to Alexandre O'Neill's notion of Portugal as a small country. However, he praises the depth of expression in the Fados and *cegadas* of Leitão de Barros's and Cottinelli's films, expressions that manage to capture something genuine 'in the dreams of the fallen woman and the seamstress whose father nominates her as a pageant queen'.

[6] Ibid., p. 53, comments that Chianca de Garcia, who was the artistic consultant for *A Canção de Lisboa*, may have played a crucial role in the film's direction. Beatriz Costa, *Sem Papas na Língua* (Mem Martins: Europa-América, 1975), p. 110, says that Chianca approached her at the São Luiz Carnival to ask her to star in the film; and that while Cottinelli was the director, Chianca 'was behind the scenes in everything'. Ribeiro, p. 277, signals Chianca de Garcia's magazine, *Imagem*, and António Lopes Ribeiro's magazine, *Kino*, as the most

Because Júlio Dantas's literature exemplifies a conservative academic tradition spanning the transition from Monarchy to Republic, Leitão de Barros's filmic adaptation of Dantas's *A Severa* perpetuates an older generation's notion of good taste.[7] In contrast, Cottinelli Telmo represents the modernity of the Futurists whose call to arms — clearly announced in 1916–17 — was to purge Portugal of such good tastes, rooted in passé manifestations of Romanticism. In fact, Cottinelli would become one of the favoured plastic artists of the SPN, under the auspices of its cultural minister, António Ferro, as the chief architect of Salazar's vision of *nacional-historicismo*, the 1940 Exposição do Mundo Português on the docks of Belém. Before that, he had designed the Portuguese Pavilion for the Exposición de Sevilla (1929), collaborated on the design and construction of Tobis Portuguesa Film Studios in Lumiar (1932), written the anthem of the Mocidade Portuguesa (1936), and illustrated the consecrated children's *ABC-zinho*.[8]

Cottinelli's most significant legacy to popular culture was his only feature-length film, *Canção*, which debuted on 7 November 1933, a little over a week after Salazar and Ferro's inauguration of the SPN, on 26 October.[9] The pioneer sound film marked a period of technological progress and modernity for Salazar's young regime, yet its cinema premiere came in right under the wire of Ferro's decree for Portuguese aesthetics that declared the plastic arts as the great showpiece of the State's identity, and promoted the arts' subservience to nationalistic ideologies.[10]

M. Félix Ribeiro remarks that '*A Canção de Lisboa*, without a doubt, created Portuguese cinema.'[11] João Bénard da Costa calls *A Canção de Lisboa* one of the best European comedies of the 1930s and one of the best Portuguese films of

vehement advocates for the construction of a talkies studio in Portugal in 1930.

[7] Ibid., p. 323, cites a critic from the *Diário Ilustrado* whose criticism of *A Canção de Lisboa* reflects his appreciation of Leitão de Barros's upholding of conservative traditions: '[*A Canção de Lisboa* has a] stupid plot, mediocre direction, inconsistent acting, decent filming and quality sound, all accompanied by songs fit for musical reviews of questionable taste. Oh! What nostalgia for *A Severa!...*'

[8] José Stuart Carvalhais introduced the *ABC-zinho*, a popular children's comic magazine, in the 1920s.

[9] Ferro's speech from the SPN's inauguration ceremony on 26 October 1933 appears in António Ferro, *Teatro e Cinema* (Lisbon: SNI, 1950), pp. 1–12; Portela, pp. 27–33, 143, dates the creation of the SPN to 1933; Bénard da Costa, p. 56, dates the institution's inauguration to 1935.

[10] See António Ferro, *Teatro e Cinema, 1936–1949* (Lisbon: SNI, 1950), pp. 1–12; Portela, p. 15; Kimberly da Costa Holton, *Performing Folkore: Ranchos Folclóricos from Lisbon to Newark* (Bloomington: Indiana University Press, 2005), p. 33. A. H. de Oliveira Marques, *History of Portugal*, II (New York: Columbia University Press, 1976), pp. 80–83, in the fall of 1929, Salazar gave a speech in which he laid the groundwork for a new constitution, and in which he first pronounced his slogan: 'Nothing against the Nation, all for the Nation.' The term Estado Novo first appeared in 1930, however we associate the beginning of the Estado Novo with the ratification of the new Constitution in 1933.

[11] Ribeiro, p. 322.

all time; a film that paved the way for all Portuguese comedies that followed.[12] The film's star, Beatriz Costa, echoes audience sentiment of nearly a half century when she calls *Canção*, 'a classic of Portuguese cinema [...] the wittiest of its kind'; and a film that 'still amuses us because of its original dialogue'.[13] However, in the scheme of the SPN's aesthetic agenda, Portugal's *nacional-cançonetismo* films — mostly light, musical comedies — would be considered the lowest of visual art forms produced during Ferro's tenure as the Minister of National Propaganda. Ferro disdained gratuitous musical interludes in film, and later declared the musical comedy 'the cancer of the Portuguese cinema'.[14] Ferro's plan for the living arts, as of 1933, would be carried out by the recently equipped Tobis Portuguesa Studios in the form of historic-folkloric movies, adaptations of nineteenth-century national literature, documentaries, and propaganda films.[15] As a result of one of the SPN's many interventions in cinematic production, *nacional-cançonetismo* films would be delayed until the 1939 release of Chianca's *Aldeia da Roupa Branca* and Leitão de Barros's *A Varanda dos Rouxinóis*.[16]

The silencing of the comic talkie indicates Portugal's limited global perspective at the time of its new constitution. The Estado Novo began to lose its sense of humour around 1936, when, despite Salazar's official neutrality in the Spanish Civil War, Lisbon, and particularly the Hotel Vitória on Avenida da Liberdade, became a refuge for Spanish Nationalists.[17] All of a sudden,

---

[12] Bénard da Costa, p. 54.

[13] Costa, *Sem Papas na Língua*, p. 110; Ibid., *Quando os Vascos Eram Santanas... e Não Só* (Mem Martins: Europa-América, 1978), p. 55, recognizes her co-stars from *Canção*, Vasco Santana and António Silva, as two of the greatest popular actors of all time.

[14] Bénard da Costa, p. 56; Ferro, *Teatro e Cinema*, pp. 62, 78, applauds Perdigão Queiroga's *Fado, História d'uma Cantadeira*, for not exploiting its musical interludes. Christine Garnier, *Salazar in Portugal: An Intimate Portrait* (New York: Farrar, Straus and Young, 1954), p. 82, in 1952, Salazar joked to his interviewer that he avoided seeing comedies because they kept him up at night and distracted him from more pressing political issues.

[15] Portela, p. 18; Bénard da Costa, p. 67, explains that 'not only did Ferro despise [comedy films], but also, not a single one of his "directives" ever favoured the genre's production.' For more on the evolution of Ferro's aesthetic agenda and his opinions of comedy films, see Ferro, *Teatro e Cinema*. Although *Canção* was shot at Lisboa Filme and given sound by Tobis Portuguesa's technology, the studio's inauguration was not celebrated until August 1934, and it was not functioning officially until 1935 when Leitão de Barros's *As Pupilas do Senhor Reitor* was filmed there. The interiors of *Gado Bravo* (1934), the third Portuguese talkie, were, like *A Severa*, filmed in Paris and given sound there. See Bénard da Costa, pp. 56–57; Ribeiro, pp. 281–82.

[16] Bénard da Costa, pp. 54–55. Between the release of *A Canção de Lisboa* and *Aldeia da Roupa Branca*, two important films featured the Fado: *Gado Bravo* (1934) and *Maria Papoila* (1937). Ribeiro, p. 399, notes that because of neglect and irresponsibility on the part of the custodians of *Varanda dos Rouxinóis* there are not any remaining copies of the film or its negative. José Leitão de Barros, *Varanda dos Rouxinóis/Vendaval Maravilhoso* (Lisbon: Cinemateca Portuguesa, n.d.) contains scripts of the two films and a preface by the author/director.

[17] Ralph Fox, *Portugal Now: Um Espião Comunista no Estado Novo* (Lisbon: Tinta-da-China,

Republican Spain was closed off as a market for Portuguese movies.[18] But the people sought escape from the austerity that dominated national cinema.[19] Box-office records account for the proliferation of films that combined simple, formulaic narratives with elements of the *comédia revisteira* to exploit the aspirations of Lisbon's middle class and poor: a recipe of popular urban settings and customs combined with spontaneous musical episodes.[20] And as the Fado, or rather, the watered-down *fado canção*, accompanied light musical theatre and the *comédia revisteira* since the 1870s, its role in the comedy film seemed already a familiar custom to the urban Portuguese audience.

The Fado had grown from the plaintive expression of the prostitutes of Lisbon's underbelly to a curiosity exhibited in noble salons, as a result of class-mingling between *fadistas* and aristocrats. In the early 1840s, the song was heard only among criminals, yet by the end of the nineteenth century, the Fado had 'decked itself out in pearls', and was heard everywhere: casinos, theatres, private parties, bullfights, and picnics.[21] In the early twentieth century, trained actors, chorus girls, and *fadistas* were interchangeable. Silent films, park openings, and gala events featured the dressed-up Fado that bore a vague resemblance to its scrappy nineteenth-century predecessor. However, despite the *fadista*'s social climbing of nearly a century, and his trading his bell-bottom trousers for a fop's overcoat, the Portuguese literary elite was unwilling to forgive him his past as a ruffian and a throwback to a nineteenth century that was better forgotten.

Before we consider the Fado's reception under the Estado Novo, we must review the diachronic evolution of the song's presence in Portuguese popular culture in the first quarter of the twentieth century. Shortly after the 1901 publication of Júlio Dantas's novel, *A Severa* and the debut of his play, *A Severa: Peça em Quatro Actos*, Pinto de Carvalho writes *História do Fado* (1903) and Alberto Pimentel publishes *A Triste Canção do Sul* (1904), two seminal books

2006), p. 36, remarks that the Hotel Vitória was an unofficial sanctuary and meeting place for Spanish Nationalists. Today the Hotel Vitória is the headquarters of the Portuguese Communist Party (PCP). Bénard da Costa, p. 55, comments: 'When, in 1936, Franco took up arms in the "crusade" that threw Spain into its Civil War, the Estado Novo lost, at the same time, its sense of humour. It hardened and took on a military character: the creation [in 1936] of the para-fascistic militias, the Legião Portuguesa [Portuguese Legion] and the Mocidade Portuguesa [Portuguese Youth], both who raised their hands, responding with 'Salazar! Salazar!' to the cry of 'Who is in Control?"

[18] Ibid., p. 68.
[19] Ibid., p. 55.
[20] Ibid, p. 67–68.
[21] António Osório, *A Mitologia Fadista* (Lisbon: Livros Horizonte, 1974), p. 51. For more on the effect of class mingling on the Fado see Michael Colvin, *The Reconstruction of Lisbon: Severa's Legacy and the Fado's Rewriting of Urban History* (Lewisburg, PA: Bucknell University Press, 2008) and 'Perdigão Queiroga's Film, *Fado, História d'uma Cantadeira*: Construction and Deconstruction of the Fado Novo', in *Portuguese Literary and Cultural Studies*, 18 (forthcoming); Alberto Pimentel, *A Triste Canção do Sul* (Lisbon: Dom Quixote, 1985); José Pinto de Carvalho, *História do Fado* (Lisbon: Dom Quixote, 1992); Rui Vieira Nery, *Para uma História do Fado* (Lisbon: Público, 2004).

about the history of the nineteenth-century Fado.[22] In 1907, Severa's guitar is honoured at a dinner in Lisbon. In 1909, André Brun's operetta, *A Severa: Ópera Cómica em Três Actos* debuts in the capital.[23] António Arroio writes his invective against the Fado, *O Canto Coral e a sua Função Social*, in 1909, to which Avelino de Sousa will respond with *O Fado e os seus Censores* (1912). In the years between, during transition to the First Republic, the magazines *O Fado* (1910) and *A Alma do Fado* (1910) appear in Lisbon. José Malhoa paints *O Fado* in 1910; the painting will be on display at the Sociedade Nacional das Belas Artes in Lisbon in 1917 before moving to the collection at the Museu da Cidade de Lisboa. In 1916, the Fado magazine, *A Canção de Portugal: O Fado* is launched and Almada Negreiros publishes the *Manifesto Anti-Dantas*. Stuart Carvalhais begins to illustrate posters and songbook covers for Sassetti publishers in 1921. In 1922, the magazine, *Guitarra de Portugal* (renamed *Ecos de Portugal* in the 1950s) appears, followed by the 1923 publication of the Fado magazine, *Canção do Sul*. Also in 1923, French director Maurice Mariaud releases the silent film, *O Fado*, adapted from Bento Mântua's play about José Malhoa's iconic painting. In 1925, Boémia, the last of the *cafés-de-camareiras*, closes. And in 1926, the year of the coup d'état and the consequent military dictatorship, Lino Ferreira's operetta, *Mouraria*, debuts in Lisbon.[24]

Prior to the military dictatorship, the Fado had penetrated popular and high-brow literature and plastic arts; it had been the concern of intellectual debates and gatherings; it had inspired serious historical studies and spawned magazines for its fans; it had projected its musical and folkloric image onto light theatre; and finally, it had debuted in film, even though its music could not be heard because sound synchronization technology had not yet been imported to Portugal.

The fact that by 1923 the Fado and the social element that the song conjures up should be the theme of a national (albeit foreign-directed) film attests to an unforeseen success in promoting the marginalized song and the marginalized social caste of its singers. M. Félix Ribeiro comments that in *O Fado*, Maurice Mariaud 'searched for and found a topic that was, without a doubt, typically Lisbon, the Fado, with all of its plebeian, dramatic atmosphere.'[25] He adds that 'for the first time in our cinematic history, the so-called national song would serve as the inspiration for a film [...] a theme so deeply rooted in Lisbon neighbourhood traditions.'[26] Mariaud's *O Fado* recognizes the autochthonous urban song as an illustration of an intriguing if un-glamorous facet of Lisbon's other realities. And in doing so, his film sets a tone that the military dictatorship

---

[22] Júlio Dantas, *A Severa: Peça em Quatro Actos* (Lisbon: Portugal-Brasil, 1931).
[23] André Brun, *A Severa: Ópera Cómica em Três Actos* (Porto: n.pub., 1912).
[24] Lino Ferreira et al., *Mouraria: Coplas da Opereta Popular em três Actos* (Lisbon: Tipografia Costa Sanches, n.d.).
[25] Ribeiro, p. 196.
[26] Ibid., p. 196.

will keep an eye on, and that the Estado Novo will piggyback on and try to control to promote its own values.

Rui Vieira Nery comments that between 1926 and 1933, 'the Fado is the object of the Dictatorship's scrutiny only within the broad context of maintaining public order and a vigilant government, without any concerns other than insuring that the musical genre and its interpreters become politically innocuous toward the status quo.'[27] As the Fado had gained popularity as a genre of protest among the working class and factory labourers in the first decades of the twentieth century, the military dictatorship was interested primarily in lyrical censorship aimed at quelling the spirit of organized strikes and the propagation of socialism, communism, and anarchy.[28] Vieira Nery elaborates that, after the 1933 inauguration of the SPN, for the regime:

> The Fado constitutes an unequivocally deplored reality with which, on a grand scale, the regime must coexist in a pragmatic manner, with the hope that the eventual advances in public education will erase, in due time, this living memory of nineteenth-century social marginality and prostitution, and, more importantly, with the certainty that a rigorous censorship of lyrics will guarantee presently the suppression of a dangerously recent tradition of texts of subversive political intervention.[29]

The evolution of the State's posture regarding the popular Fado allows us examine the Estado Novo's, and particularly the SPN's apprehensions about the song's subversive elements. The renewed totalitarian control over popular culture, initiated by António Ferro in 1933, will result in thematic censorship of films, regarding the Fado and the urban poor. As a result, Portuguese films of the 1930s and 1940s will present an innocent notion of folkloric paupers whose ambitions are curtailed by their social immobility. And necessarily, the disgruntled labourer, discontent with the so-called progress of the present, is absent from these urban vignettes. He will not reappear favourably in Portuguese film until 1952, in Perdigão Queiroga's *Madragoa*, in which he will zealously espouse a work ethic imbued with the regime's values of 'Deus, Pátria e Família'. And once again in Constantino Esteves's O Miúdo da Bica (1964), the protagonist — Fernando Farinha playing himself — suffers for having abandoned an honest living on the docks for a life of Fado, drinking, gambling and easy women.

However, *Severa* and *Canção* are not subject to the SPN's scrutiny. And as the films debut during a period of transition between the military dictatorship and the Estado Novo, they manage to fall through the cracks of censorship, and are perhaps the best examples of shrouded dissatisfaction among the lower classes; rather, *A Severa* is a story about frustration with an unjust caste system and *Canção* is a story about social climbing. In their focus on uncertain urban

---

[27] Vieira Nery, p. 219.
[28] Ibid., p.218.
[29] Ibid., p. 221.

class identity, both films reveal the underlying public disenchantment with Portugal's recent versions of democracy. As the Fado is present in moments of social struggle, it accompanies the films' diverse perspectives on class in Lisbon. And as such themes will be voiced by artists and intellectuals in the 1930s, thus arises the question of the Fado's viability as the soundtrack to a modern regime.

By the 1930s, the Fado, controversially considered Portugal's national song, was at the centre of the tug-of-war between tardo-Romanticism and the SPN's modernizing aesthetics.[30] The Fado posed a threat to the Estado Novo because it glorified the past as it criticized the progress of the present. Salazar disliked the Fado because he believed it had a 'softening influence on the Portuguese character,' and it '[sapped] all energy from the soul and [led] to inertia'.[31] The original goals of the SPN to 'combat defeatism' met one of their biggest challenges with the popularity of the Fado that, in 1936, Luís Moita would call the 'canção de vencidos' [song of the vanquished].[32] Thus, the Fado, the most recognizable ornament on the façade of Portuguese culture, 'what the outsider [saw] when looking in', was characterized by defeat.[33]

But let us not forget that Ferro had been a member of the Orpheu generation whose call to arms was to purge dominant conservative Portuguese literary and artistic tastes of tardo-Romanticism.[34] The Fado reeked of nineteenth-century aesthetics and, therefore, should have been part of that purgation. Nevertheless, the Fado's popularity had become such that, even before the 1933 inauguration of the SPN, Salazar's government had no choice but to make the song — with concessions — a part of the consecrated national repertoire. Through an orderly censorship, the Estado Novo would ensure that the already popular Fado did not blatantly contradict the regime's notion of progress; and by promoting the *pobrete mas alegrete* [poor but happy] images of Lisbon's *fadistas* and their degraded popular neighbourhoods, the government kept the potentially subversive song

---

[30] Colvin, *The Reconstruction of Lisbon*, studies the Fado's problematical relationship with Portuguese Fascism.

[31] Garnier, p. 190.

[32] António Ferro, *Catorze Anos de Política do Espírito* (Lisbon: SNI, 1948), p. 21; Portela, p. 30. See Luís Moita, *O Fado: Canção de Vencidos* (Lisbon: n.pub., 1936).

[33] Ferro, *Salazar*, p. 86; Portela, p. 15.

[34] The Orpheu generation refers to the group of artists and writers who contributed to the avant-garde *Orpheu* magazine during the early decades of the twentieth century. The most prominent figures of this intellectual circle were Mário de Sá-Carneiro, Fernando Pessoa, and José de Almada Negreiros. António Ferro was not in the intellectual foreground of the Orpheu's modernizing aesthetics, but he was active within the group, and the influence of the Portuguese Futurists is palpable in Ferro's proposals for a nationalistic aesthetics. See Portela, p. 20; Selles Paes, *Da Arte Moderna em Portugal* (Lisbon: SNI, 1962), p. 35. Ferro's son, António Quadros, called his father an apostle and a missionary for the Orpheu generation, and attributes to him the national and international divulgence and institutionalization of the group's intellectual agenda. See Portela, p. 19; António Quadros, *António Ferro* (Lisbon: SNI, 1963), pp. viii–ix.

at bay.³⁵ Through comedy film, and later, urban folkloric films, the regime would market the Fado as a tool to identify Lisbon's poor as a happy people, and the *pobrete mas alegrete* trope would haunt these genres well into the 1960s with films such as O *Pátio das Cantigas* (1942), O *Costa do Castelo* (1943), *A Menina da Rádio* (1944), *Fado, História d'uma Cantadeira* (1947), *Rosa de Alfama* (1953), and O *Miúdo da Bica* (1964).³⁶

However, because the production of *A Severa* and *A Canção de Lisboa* preceded the foundation of the SPN, these films are privileged. They are the only Portuguese talkies of the period that escaped Ferro's decree that upheld that, thereafter, Portuguese artistic production would be: 'For everyone else, and for us, an answer for everything and the only path, the supreme cry, that no longer will signify one man's name, but the synthesis of a redeeming idea, the symbol of a greater system: Salazar!'³⁷ And as *Canção* is Portugal's second talkie, it allows us to spy its mocking satire of *A Severa*, as it laughs at the expense of Portugal's aesthetic downfall, *saudosismo*.

From the beginning of Cottinelli Telmo's film, the crossroads between tradition and modernity is announced in the credits to Tobis Portuguesa Studio's debut film. Our last silent image before the first incursion of sound in a Portuguese film is of an Art-deco rendering of the Republic's anti-Semitic blazon: a solid white box, surrounded by seven castles of the eleven that Afonso Henriques conquered from the Moors on the way to the Battle of Ourique.³⁸ The white box contains the five *quinas* [scutcheons] that represent Christ's five wounds, and that contain the thirty coins for which the Jews sold Christ to the Romans. But the *quinas* lose their metaphorical value, as they no longer appear as warrior's shields; rather, they look like five-point dice, dominoes, or even Lego pieces. A new era of technology, signalled by Portugal's first sound-film

---

³⁵ I shared these opinions with journalist, John Lewis, 'Tainted Love', *The Guardian* (London), 27 April 2007, 3, p. 5. Ruben de Carvalho, *Um Século de Fado* (Alfragide: Ediclube, 1999), p. 88, comments on the general will of dictators to attract popular support, and that the popular Fado, 'did not constitute a phenomenon generated by Fascism; rather, because of its popularity, it was courted by [the regime] — and with some success.'

³⁶ Daniel Melo, *Salazarismo e Cultura Popular (1933–1958)* (Lisbon: Imprensa de Ciências Sociais, 2001), p. 114, indicates that the Junta Central de Casas de Povo (JCCP), a body that promoted rural cultural centres with the goal of propagating a Portuguese nationalism rooted in an agricultural past and present, opposed the notion of the happy but poor urban citizens. He cites the JCCP's use of cinema in the Casas de Povo, in 1945, as an '[instrument] of popular education and culture', and he remarks on the JCCP's selection and promotion of what they deemed 'adequate films', and their rejection of films that 'might constitute a perversion of good habits and social order [especially those that alluded to] the dream of an easy and happy life in the city.'

³⁷ Ferro, *Catorze Anos de Política do Espírito*, p. 21; Portela, p. 30.

³⁸ In Cottinelli Telmo's film, we see a silent image before we hear any sound. However, in Leitão de Barros's film, the novelty of sound is celebrated in isolation. Before we see the images of Severa's gypsy caravan on the plains of the Ribatejo, we are confronted with a black screen and an overture by Frederico de Freitas.

studio warrants a new and renewed sense of nationalism: a modern, progressive Portugal that never loses sight of its fight for autonomy — dating back to Guimarães in 1128, when Afonso Henriques challenged his mother, the Pope, and Leonese political authorities in his declaration of Portuguese independence. Tobis Portuguesa Studio's inauguration of sound film, with *Canção*, means technological modernity and independence for Portugal. Portugal may now produce her own movies, in her own studios, free from French technology. The Franco-Portuguese production of Leitão de Barros's *A Severa*, two years earlier, seems like a compromise as we behold the first Portuguese talkie, made by the Portuguese, in Portugal![39]

But Leitão de Barros's successful *A Severa* is the mould for all *fadista* films produced thereafter. And incarnations of Dina Teresa Moreira's interpretation of Maria Severa are palpable in Hermínia Silva's role as Maria da Luz in *Aldeia da Roupa Branca*; in Amália Rodrigues's sombre portrayals of Ana Maria in *Fado, História d'uma Cantadeira,* and as Amália in *Les Amants du Tage*; and in Rosa Silvestre's forgettable Lena in *Rosa de Alfama*. Nevertheless, when the filmic Severa appears unexpectedly in *Canção*, invoked by the corpulent Vasco Leitão (Vasco Santana), we are obliged to examine the dialogue between Cottinelli's and Leitão de Barros's films.

The most prominent of the remaining publicity posters that José de Almada Negreiros designed for *A Canção de Lisboa* establishes a direct dialogue with Leitão de Barros's *A Severa*, by flaunting its status as the more nationalistic product of the first two talkies.[40] Almada's poster announces *Canção* as 'o primeiro filme português feito por portugueses' [the first Portuguese film made by the Portuguese], and thus challenges Leitão de Barros's movie poster that calls his film, 'o mais português dos filmes portugueses' [the most Portuguese of Portuguese films].[41] Furthermore, Almada's depiction of *Canção*'s protagonist,

[39] Ribeiro, p. 281, comments that at the conference of the Sociedade Universal de Superfilmes (SUS), on 6 August 1930, dedicated to the problem of building a sound-film studio in Portugal, Leitão de Barros spoke of the 'real advantages' of Portugal's being able to produce her own talkies, and he continued to elaborate on his own plans for Portugal's first talkie, *A Severa*.

[40] Rui Estrela *A Publicidade no Estado Novo*, 2 vols (Lisbon: Simplesmente Comunicando, 2004), I: *1932–1959*, p. 74, notes that Almada Negreiros's poster for the Pavilhão Português at the Exposición de Sevilla (1929) — for which Cottinelli Temo had been the principal architect — won the fair's award for best poster.

[41] Bénard da Costa, p. 52, explains that Leitão de Barros, aware of his own limitations, asked for René Clair's help on *A Severa*. Clair was not interested, so he gave the task to his assistant, Bernard Brunius. As the publicity for *A Severa* often mentioned Clair's supervision of the project, rumours spread that 'the film was more his than Leitão de Barros's'. Ribeiro, p. 282, says that Clair and Brunius worked with Leitão de Barros, at Clair's house in St. Tropez, and that Brunius followed the Portuguese cinematographer to Lisbon, where they worked through September 1930 on planning and preparing the film. Ribeiro, pp. 318–20, remarks that because the Tobis Portuguesa Sound Film Studios were new to Portugal, only being initiated there with *A Canção de Lisboa*, foreign technicians aided in the early stages of production; however, many of the foreign employees turned the work that they had started

Vasco's playing a Portuguese guitar mocks Leitão de Barros's movie poster's earnest image of Dina Teresa Moreira as the pitiable Mouraria prostitute, Maria Severa, as she plays the *guitarra*, preparing to 'die embracing the Fado'.[42] The two figures are posed in a similar manner, and their silhouettes are almost identical, as Vasco's robust frame mimics Severa's excessive layering of gypsy scarves and skirts.[43] During the turning point in *Canção*, when Vasco sobers up, passes his medical-school exams with distinction, and gives his final Fado performance to an avid audience at the Retiro do Alexandrino, the camera focuses on a faiance-tile image of Vasco. In the portrait, the *fadista*-turned-doctor poses with his Portuguese guitar, and now, his scholarly gown fills out the silhouette that alludes to Dina Teresa's attitude as Severa.[44]

But Almada's involvement in *A Canção de Lisboa* may be more politically compromising than his poster's jab at Leitão de Barros's cinematic adaptation of Júlio Dantas's novel and play. Rather, it stirs up an old aesthetic rivalry and ideological schism that echoes the Estado Novo's tug-of-war between a discourse of tradition and progress: the battle between the Futurists and the regenerative and degenerative nineteenth century that rears its ailing, nostalgic head to alert us of Portugal's disenchantment with the Republic.

'Morram os fadistas!' [down with the *fadistas*!] a drunk Vasco Leitão shouts in the hilarious climactic scene of *A Canção de Lisboa*. Cottinelli Telmo borrows the language of Almada Negreiros's proto-Futurist *Manifesto Anti-Dantas* (1916) that parodies António Arroio's anti-Fado tirades in O *Canto Coral e a sua Função Social* (1909), which urge the Portuguese to abandon the Fado for erudite music.[45] However, with satirical, yet targeted, exclamations like 'a generation that allows itself to be represented by a Dantas is a generation that never was!' and 'a generation with a Dantas in the saddle is an impotent donkey!', Almada's

---

over to their Portuguese counterparts without any compromise to the quality of the film.

[42] 'Novo Fado da Severa (Rua do Capelão)', Júlio Dantas/ Frederico de Freitas.

[43] Leitão de Barros's poster identifies Maria Severa as a Gypsy, following the erroneous lead of Dantas's novel, in which Severa's mother, Barbuda, flees Spain in a Gypsy caravan to settle in Lisbon's Mouraria. Maria Severa Onofriana was born in Anjos, and when she was very young she lived on Rua de Vicente Borga (Rua da Madragoa). Her parents, like most inhabitants of nineteenth-century Madragoa, were probably migrants from Ovar or Estarreja.

[44] It is an interesting coincidence that in 1933, before she moved to Rio de Janeiro, Dina Teresa had given her farewell performance at the Retiro da Severa, at the recently completed Parque Eduardo VII. The Retiro do Alexandrino — which alludes to the Retiro da Severa — appears to be set in the Parque do Príncipe Real. Ribeiro, p. 286, attributes Dina Teresa's initial visit to Brazil as an obligation to 'receive the warm applauses of the audience that had celebrated her performance [in the role of Severa].'

[45] António Arroio, O *Canto Coral e a sua Função Social* (Coimbra: n.pub., 1909); José de Almada Negreiros, *Manifesto Anti-Dantas* (Lisbon: n.pub., 1916). Afonso Lopes Vieira, *Em Demanda do Graal* (Lisbon: SNI, 1946), p. 352, denies the Fado's status as a national song, calls it a 'lyrical embarrassment', and declares that it is 'only Lisbon's song'. Perhaps Cottinelli's title mocks Lopes Vieira's declaration.

Manifesto's point is clear.[46] Like Arroio's invectives that blame the popularity of the Fado for Portugal's anachronistic cultural under-development in the context of a modern twentieth-century Europe, Almada's gripes attribute Portuguese society's backward character to its perpetuation of tardo-Romanticism, and signals Dantas as the scapegoat for the Nation's consecration of hackneyed interpretations of a nineteenth-century Portugal.[47] By putting Dantas at the 'prow [of the] canoe on dry land' — as he sarcastically calls Portugal's literary elite — Almada's *Manifesto Anti-Dantas* assumes a new face in the early 1930s at the moment when Leitão de Barros's film resurrects Dantas's *A Severa*, thus making tardo-Romanticism relevant for Portuguese audiences fifteen years after the ushering in of Futurism. In fact, because the reception of Leitão de Barros's *A Severa* is so successful at the box office — over 200,000 tickets sold during its six-month run in Portuguese cinemas — Dantas's generation, or as Almada calls them, 'the coven of indigents, losers, blind men [...] charlatans, and sellouts', is an even bigger menace to Futurism in the first half of the 1930s than when Almada wrote his *Manifesto* in 1917. At the dawn of the era of the Estado Novo, when the SPN will be force-feeding an aesthetics of progress to Portugal, the people close their mouths and feast on nostalgic memories of the nineteenth century, and look to Dantas's literature for their cultural cues.

But whereas Cottinelli's film is the first and last Portuguese musical comedy of the pre-SPN era, its dialogue with Leitão de Barros's *A Severa* adheres — perhaps inadvertently — to the very aesthetics proposed by Ferro, despite the cultural minister's negation of such comedy as appropriate for the Estado Novo's national heritage. That is, through *Canção*'s parody of *A Severa*, we witness the rebirth of Portuguese cinema. And as a result of the film's shrouded proposal to put the folkloric nineteenth century to rest, a twentieth-century folklore is born, even if only for a moment.

The opening music of *A Canção de Lisboa* announces the ringing out of an old Lisbon to make way for a new one: the satiric theme that underlines the film's dialogue with *A Severa*. 'A Canção de Lisboa' sings Lisbon's praises rooted in the city's natural endowments: 'Cidade Jardim / Que o Tejo azul vem beijar

---

[46] It is an interesting coincidence that Almada Negreiros's *Manifesto* is illustrated with a series of pointing hands to indicate paragraph breaks, and that Cottinelli's camera focuses on a reproduction of the same illustration, pointing the audience to the Retiro do Alexandrino, where Vasco has become a famous *fadista*. Costa, *Sem Papas na Língua*, pp. 140–42, narrates her encounter with Júlio Dantas when she was invited by António Ferro to discuss with Salazar an African tour in which she and Vasco Santana would be the stars. The actress remarks that her circle at the café A Brasileira — which included Almada Negreiros — delighted in her story, 'in light of the *Manifesto Anti-Dantas*'.

[47] Portela, pp. 24, 76; Quadros, p. 13, signal that, in 1922, António Ferro refers to Dantas as 'the coiffeur of mediocre spirits'. Despite Ferro's apparent disdain for Dantas's tardo-Romanticism, the Minister of National Propaganda appoints Dantas as President of the Executive Committee for the Exposição do Mundo Português — in which Almada Negreiros collaborates as a decorative painter — in an attempt to bridge the irreconcilable aesthetics of two generations.

/ Sua saudade sem fim, de te deixar' [City of Gardens / That the blue Tagus comes ashore to kiss / The River feels infinitely wistful for having to leave your side].[48] The camera pans above the Terreiro do Paço to show the order of the Pombaline Reconstruction, and the grandeur of the city's monuments alongside the progress of the electric trams. Then we are transported to a veranda in the Customs House overlooking naval ships in the Tagus estuary: 'Tudo em ti prende e seduz / Até o céu tem mais cor / E o sol mais luz' [Everything about you captivates and seduces / Even your skies are bluer / And your sun brighter]. From here, we leave modern Lisbon to travel to a humble capital of seventeenth-century working-class homes. We witness the typical morning of the urban dwellers in the fictitious Bairro dos Castelinhos that evokes any of Lisbon's riverside neighbourhoods: Alfama, Bica, Graça, Madragoa, even Mouraria: 'Alegre como um pregão / Acordas sempre a cantar / A linda canção do teu despertar' [Light and happy like the hearkening of a fishmonger / You wake up singing / Your beautiful reveille]. And in her *cantiga d'amigo*, the singer reminds us that this precious, unrivalled city is 'the flower of Portugal'.

But then the *fadista*'s peaceful homage to Lisbon's splendour shifts from a ballad reminiscent of a *fado canção* to a ragtime sung by an all-male barbershop quartet. Lisbon's beauty is forgotten, as the song's lyrics incorporate the medieval Galician-Portuguese tradition of *leixa-pren* [give and take] and assume the candour and mordancy of a *cantiga d'escarnho e maldizer* to focus on the characterization of Vasco Leitão, the film's (other) protagonist:

> Tu vais ficar mal, mandrião
> No teu exame final
> Vais ver ó Leitão,
> No teu exame final
> Vais ficar mal, mandrião
> Vais ver ó Leitão
> Vais ficar mal
>
> [You're going to fail, you lazy bum
> Your final exam
> You'll see, Leitão
> Your final exam
> You're going to fail, you lazy bum
> You'll see, Leitão
> You're going to fail.]

And as Vasco runs late through the hills of Estefânia to the Medical College, he pushes out of his way a *varina* — the incarnation of the nineteenth-century folkloric Lisbon, the very fishmonger who sings Lisbon's reveille! As Vasco makes his way through traffic on his way to Campo de Sant'Ana, we imagine the horns of the new automobiles waking up a modern Lisbon where the *varina* soon will be an anachronism, and her 'Ó Viva da Costa', a colourful memory of our grandparents.

---

[48] 'A Canção de Lisboa', José Galhardo/ Raul Portela and Raul Ferrão.

Leitão de Barros exploits Lisbon folklore, deeply rooted in nineteenth-century popular and aristocratic traditions. The three mainstays of the 'verdadeiro poema de raça' [the true poem of the Portuguese race] — as the movie poster dubs *A Severa* — are the bullfight at the arena in Algés; Severa's Fado performances for the nobility at the gardens of the Marquesa de Seide, and in her agony in the Mouraria; and the march of St Anthony's feast that continues to take place in the Mouraria during and immediately after Severa's death.[49] In a similar manner, three comical moments mark the plot of Cottinelli's film, but with parodies of such Lisbon traditions: Vasco's classmates satirize a bullfight when his aunts arrive at the train station in the Rossio; Vasco and Alice improvise a *festa popular* [popular urban festival] reminiscent of St Anthony's or St John's feast as part of their courtship ceremony;[50] and the Lisbon Fado marks the turning point during which a drunk Vasco degrades the Fado, and as he sobers up, becomes a *fadista* and an exemplary student, and shortly thereafter, renounces the Fado and becomes a doctor.

Nevertheless, we are not interested in Cottinelli's recontextualization of Leitão de Barros's urban folklore merely for the content of such scenes; rather, Cottinelli's re-enactment of three pivotal episodes, filmed with sound, outdoors in Portugal, show off the 1933 film's technological progress in comparison to the 1931 film. And as the audience remembers Leitão de Barros's recent movie, and logically has expectations for the recognizable folkloric tropes, Cottinelli's thwarting of such expectations forces the audience to perceive aesthetic and social progress in *A Canção de Lisboa*: notions that were not only absent, but even disdained in *A Severa*.

Leitão de Barros's movie poster announces *A Severa*'s 'aparatosa espera de toiros' [over-the-top pre-bullfight show] and 'monumental corrida' [monumental bullfight]. Nevertheless, during these dramatic and seemingly infinite outdoor scenes, if it were not for the synchronized sound and score, added later at studios in Paris, we would be stuck in the era of Portuguese silent films. The images are reminiscent of Aurélio da Paz dos Reis's *Feira do Gado na Corujeira* (1896), João Freire Correia's *Batalha de Flores no Campo Grande* (1907), and *Portugal Desportivo* (anonymous, 1917), in their documentation of sporting events.[51] Nevertheless, we forgive Leitão de Barros the technological

---

[49] The summer traditions of the bullfights and of the 13 June St Anthony's feast, occurring on the day and evening of Severa's fatal collapse, stray from biography, as the *fadista* died on 30 November (1846).

[50] The trope of St John's feast returns most remarkably in Armando de Miranda's *Capas Negras* (1947) in which Amália Rodrigues and Alberto Ribeiro sing a *desgarrada* around a bonfire.

[51] In July 2008, the Cinemateca Portuguesa–Museu de Cinema in Lisbon presented *O Cinema Português de 1896 a 1918*, a three-part series of Portuguese silent films. Ribeiro, pp. 17–20, relates that in 1940, Luís Nunes and he went to Porto to speak to Aurélio da Paz dos Reis's son regarding a retrospective of his father's pioneer filmmaking. They returned to Lisbon with a decayed copy of the film, *Saída do Pessoal Operário da Fábrica Confiança* (1896),

lag, and appreciate the beauty of the cinematography and the novelty of the musical accompaniment. However, even critics who laud the innovative film, comment on the poor synchronization of sound during the few moments when the characters speak, principally when Custódia throws himself in front of the bull to prove his love for Severa.

Similarly, in Cottinelli's film, when Vasco's aunts arrive from Trás-os-Montes at the Central Station in the Rossio, we are reminded of the origins of motion pictures in Lisbon.[52] English filmmaker, Henry Short's *Portuguese Railway Train* (1896) is the first documented moving image ever shot in Portugal. The short film — less than two minutes long — captures the arrival of the first train from Cascais at the Cais do Sodré.[53] In *A Canção de Lisboa*, we watch the trains arrive, and as the old ladies descend onto the platform, they give evidence of Portugal's technological progress. They have travelled to the Southern capital from the most remote of continental Portugal's regions; and unlike the elegant local travellers of Henry Short's film, we hear them speaking as they greet Vasco.

However, as Vasco and his aunts leave the station and enter Rossio Square, a move from indoors to outdoors, we remark on the transition in sound — although not seamless — as our characters continue speaking: impossible two years earlier, when Leitão de Barros had to dub such scenes, resulting in obvious distinctions between the quality of indoor and outdoor scenes in *A Severa*. But just in case the audience has forgotten the technical problems with recent sound film in Portugal, Vasco's classmates arrive in the Rossio, in a *traquitanas* [a beaten-up old carriage] on their way home from a bullfight à la Leitão de Barros! The aunt's comply with their characterization as incarnations of an old Portugal, the nineteenth-century Trás-os-Montes that swoons when it comes in contact with the fast-paced, chaotic twentieth-century Lisbon, where car engines and horns spook horses and old ladies alike. The aunts faint, and are taken, unconscious, to their hotels in a comically dramatic procession that simultaneously rivals Leitão de Barros's 'aparatosa espera de toiros', and mocks Severa's fainting spell outside the bullring: the Romantic adumbration of her final breath.

---

and ten metres of the film, *Feira na Corujeira* (1896). A friend of Nunes, Eugène Shufftan, suggested a laboratory where the films' defects could be restored. Ribeiro hesitated regarding *Saída*, and he only turned *Feira na Corujeira* over to Shufftan. Ribeiro speculates that most of *Feira na Corujeira* was lost in a laboratory in New York. All that remains of *Feira na Corujeira* is a fragment made up of nine photograms.

[52] In light of the filmed grandeur of the arrival at the Central Station, we must overlook the fact that trains coming from Trás-os-Montes do not come in to the Rossio.

[53] Tiago Baptista, 'O Cinema Português de 1896 a 1918' (Cinemateca Portuguesa–Museu do Cinema, 3 July 2008), Henry Short's *Portuguese Railway station/Chegada ao Cais do Sodré do Primeiro Comboio de Cascais* is one of the first films ever shot in Portugal, and is part of his series, *A Tour in Spain and Portugal*, that appeared in London on 22 October 1897.

Leitão de Barros's film ends on a sad note: Severa dies in the arms of her lover, while singing the Fado. In the film, Marialva hands Severa her *guitarra*, and she sings César das Neves's 'Canção da Desgraçada':

> Quem tiver filhas no mundo
> Não fale das desgraçadas
> As filhas da desgraça
> Também nasceram honradas[54]
>
> [Whoever has daughters in this world
> Don't speak ill of disgraced women
> For the daughters of disgrace
> Were born honourable too.]

Halfway through the verse Severa coughs, and expires in Marialva's arms. As Marialva closes the *fadista*'s eyes, revellers continue to celebrate St Anthony's feast in a poorly synchronized musical scene in which they abandon the Mouraria, as their bonfire extinguishes, and the film ends.[55] In Cottinelli's film, the *festa popular* marks the courtship of Vasco and Alice. We witness, for the first time in Portuguese cinema, a spontaneous musical interlude with all of the fanfare of a Hollywood adaptation of a Broadway musical. The celebrants march to the tune of the *Fungagá*, 'O Balãozinho', as the choruses join in to complement Vasco and Alice's duet, a song that carries the audience ahead through the plot of the film.[56]

Nevertheless, the appearance of the seemingly gratuitous *festa popular* in *A Canção de Lisboa* constitutes an evolution in Portuguese film towards the aesthetics of the *comedia revisteira* with all of the artificial sophistication of American talkies like *The Jazz Singer* (1927) and *42nd Street* (1933): an aesthetics that will be perpetuated in Portugal well into the 1960s to the chagrin of

---

[54] 'Canção da Desgraçada (Fado Choradinho)', César das Neves/ A. Branco. Colvin, *The Reconstruction of Lisbon*, p. 119 n. 10, remarks, 'In Dantas, *A Severa*, 237, a *fadista* sings from [Sousa do Casacão's] 'Fado da Severa': 'Chorai, fadistas chorai / Que a Severa já morreu' [Cry, *fadistas* cry / For Severa is dead] during Severa's funeral procession. In Dantas, *A Severa; Peça em Quatro Actos*, a chorus of *fadistas* sings the verse when Severa collapses (200). Dantas, however, must resort to ellipsis to avoid anachronism, as the previous lines of the 'Fado da Severa' would read: 'Hoje mesmo faz um ano / Que a Severa faleceu' [A year ago today / Severa died].'

[55] 'Quando a Severa Morreu', António Vilar da Costa / Júlio Proença, alludes to the final scene in Leitão de Barros's film in its narration of Severa's death during a *festa popular*: 'Noite fagueira / São João na Mouraria / Uma fogueira / Arde no Largo da Guia' [A pleasant evening / Saint John's Feast in the Mouraria / A bonfire / Burns in Largo da Guia]; and again, 'Mas já no Largo / A fogueira se extinguia / Destino amargo / Severa não mais viria / Àquela hora / Nos braços do seu amado / Cantava agora / O seu derradeiro fado' [But in the Largo / The bonfire burned out / A bitter fate / Severa wasn't going to show up / At that moment / In the arms of her lover / She sang / Her final Fado]. Colvin, *The Reconstruction of Lisbon*, pp. 48–68, examines the re-setting of Severa's death in various media.

[56] 'O Balãozinho', José Galhardo/ Raul Portela and Raul Ferrão.

the SPN/SNI (Secretariado Nacional de Informação/National Secretariat of Information), and, ironically, of those who will view *nacional-cançonetismo* films as the Estado Novo's opium for the masses.[57] This evolution evident in Cottinelli's re-setting of the *festa popular*, however, does not necessarily imply a criticism of his predecessor's scene; rather, it constitutes a homage to how far Portuguese cinema has come — since the filming of *Festas de São Torcato em Guimarães* (anonymous, 1912), for example — even if Portuguese film will not progress so much in the next thirty years.[58] That is, the scene of the *festa popular* in *A Canção de Lisboa* recognizes the innovation of *A Severa*'s final scene, and continues the innovation made possible by Leitão de Barros's pioneer film.

But let us return to the final scene in *A Severa*, when Marialva hands the *fadista* the *guitarra* so that she may sing her last words. The episode constitutes a Romantic ending to one of Portugal's most consecrated late-Romantic works of literature, Dantas's novel, *A Severa*, and his play, *A Severa: Peça em Quatro Actos*. Severa struggles futilely for a love that she can never realize, because she is a prostitute and Marialva an aristocrat. When the lovers become aware of the strength of their passion, against the social odds, it is too late: Severa dies of a vague disease that involves fainting, swooning, and coughing. The Romantic tubercular death, made famous on screen five years later by Greta Garbo in *Camille* (1936), debuts in Portugal as the conclusion to its first sound film. The audience is moved by the ending, but the new intellectual elite identifies the outdated trope, and mocks the nineteenth century that resists being extinguished like the very flickering bonfire flame with which Leitão de Barros's film closes.

A Canção de Lisboa recognizes the popularity of the Fado, from the recent success of *A Severa*, and incorporates the controversial national song into the film's plot. Toward the end of Cotinelli's film, Vasco and his colleague, Carlos (Manoel de Oliveira), are drinking at the Retiro do Alexandrino, where Maria Albertina is singing a *fado mouraria*, 'Fado dos Beijos Quentes'. Unlike Severa's reverent audience of paupers in the Mouraria, or the genteel aristocrats who marvel at the novelty of the lowly song when Severa sings at the Marchioness's gardens, Maria Albertina's public, like the singer herself, is strictly middle class.[59] Their behaviour before the Fado performance is learned: it is neither the

---

[57] Bénard da Costa, p. 67, comments: 'Often, it was said simplistically that [the musical films of the 1940s] were symbols of national escapism, the beloved children of a regime that did its best to make 'real problems' vanish from the screens, and that exploited them like the three F's of its propaganda (Fado, Futebol, and Fátima) as the opium of the masses. They would be, above all, the films of the Estado Novo. Such an explanation is not accurate.'

[58] *Festas de São Torcato em Guimarães* was part of the Cinemateca Portuguesa–Museu do Cinema's July 2008 programme of silent films, *O Cinema Português de 1896 a 1918*.

[59] Eduardo Sucena, *Lisboa, o Fado e os Fadistas* (Lisbon: Vega, 2002), p. 227, traces a biography of Maria Albertina Soares da Paiva, in which we learn that the *fadista* was of humble *varina* origins. However, by 1933, she was already famous from her recordings and her appearance in the operetta *História do Fado* (1931). She would achieve some international

manifestation of a communal fate of the urban poor, nor is the disenchantment of a parasitic *fidalguia* witnessing, for the first time, the suffering of their inferiors. Rather, the Fado has gone mainstream, and ceases to characterize a class, as it moulds itself to the tastes of all Portuguese in a democratic, if unstable Republic.[60]

But Cottinelli Telmo was on the cutting edge of architecture, design, and aesthetics, and ran in circles concentric to the Orpheu generation who disdained what the mainstream had become in Portugal. The fact that Maria Albertina's staid Fado performance — similar to Dina Teresa's re-enactment of Severa's performances of nearly a century earlier — is contemporary mainstream taste in Portugal is problematic to a new generation of intellectuals who want to bury the nineteenth century and get on with the twentieth. Vasco's drunken repudiation of Maria Albertina's performance manifests the will of the Orpheu generation, by satirizing, yet declaring, Almada Negreiros's anti-Dantas, and by association, anti-nineteenth century and anti-*fadista* diatribes.

Furthermore, because fairly recently *fadistófilos* had argued over the authenticity of Maria Severa's Portuguese guitar — a *guitarra* that would become national heritage on permanent display at the Museu da Cidade de Lisboa in Campo Grande — Vasco commits a sacrilege when he grabs the instrument from Maria Albertina's accompanist.[61] We expect that Vasco will start playing a *guitarrada*, but our expectations are thwarted when Vasco uses the Portuguese guitar as a tennis racket to beat away the projectiles that the public tosses at him: the angry audience that defends Portugal's will to sit passive — albeit by way of violent protest — entertained by filmic and musical regurgitations of light literature and popular song that should have disappeared, at least, a decade earlier. And in Vasco's irreverent tennis match, and in his act of destroying the *guitarra*, Severa's Lisbon, that persists thanks to Dantas and Leitão de Barros, is rendered inefficient, passée, useless, dead!

However, a simple rejection of the tastes of the masses will not suffice: neither for Cottinelli Telmo, nor for the Estado Novo. We have mentioned that despite the incongruity of the nineteenth-century Fado as the soundtrack to a Modernist, rather, Futurist regime, the SPN will recognize the propagandistic value of courting the masses at their level. And just as the Estado Novo will give in, reluctantly, and promote, but seldom praise, *fadista* and *nacional-cançonetismo* films, Cottinelli Telmo sees the value of not alienating his audience — the same audience that made *A Severa* a box-office smash — and not favouring the

---

recognition, giving performances in Spain, Argentina, the United States and Canada. Melo, pp. 216–17, mentions that Maria Albertina, invited by the SPN, represented Lisbon at the 1937 World's Fair in Paris, singing the Fado.

[60] Colvin, *The Reconstruction of Lisbon*, pp. 76–77; Osório, p. 24; Vieira Nery, p. 60.
[61] Joaquim Pais de Brito, *Fado: Vozes de Sombras* (Lisbon: Electa, 1994), p. 144; António Manuel Morais, *Fado e Tauromaquia no Séc. XIX* (Lisbon: Hugin, 2003), pp. 178–81, refer to the controversy over the 1907 dinner to honour Severa's *guitarra*.

dogmatism of a generation of intellectuals whose impact has been considerably less popular than Dantas's and Leitão de Barros's singing 'gypsy harlot'.[62]

In Portugal, the advent of the Estado Novo, the inauguration of the regime's publicity machine — António Ferro's SPN — and the birth of Portuguese talkies coincide in the early 1930s. The first half of the decade is characterized by a move toward ideological, aesthetic, and technological progress. Nevertheless, that progress is mediated by a contradictory current of tradition rooted in distorted memories of a Romantic nineteenth century. The Estado Novo's will toward austere modernity conflicts with the masses' nostalgia for the fantasy of stability under the Monarchy: a fantasy problematized by the succession of unsustainable Republics between 1910 and the 1930s.

The conflict between progress and tradition is evident in the dialogue between Portugal's first talkies, Leitão de Barros's *A Severa* and Cottinelli Telmo's *A Canção de Lisboa*: a dialogue that mimics the tension between the Futurists and the tardo-Romanticists. Whereas Leitão de Barros's film — and by association, Júlio Dantas's drama and novel from which the film is adapted — promotes nostalgia for the nineteenth century, and rejects the progress of the nascent regime, Cottinelli Telmo's comedy embraces an ideology of progress by parodying the earlier film. Almada Negreiros's movie poster for *A Canção de Lisboa* pays homage to *A Severa* to draw our attention to the status of Cottinelli's film as the 'first Portuguese film made by the Portuguese'. In *Canção*, twentieth-century Republican class mobility — incarnate in Vasco who vacillates between being an heir to a small trust fund, a failing medical student, a *fadista*, a drunkard, and a doctor — contrasts with *A Severa*'s nineteenth-century caste system in which nobility have semi-clandestine relationships with the prostitutes from Lisbon's slums. Furthermore, Cottinelli Telmo appropriates Leitão de Barros's folkloric tropes of the bullfight, the *festa popular*, and the Fado, not only to underscore how far Portuguese sound film has progressed since the operation of Tobis Portuguesa Studios in 1933, but also to remark on the director's continuation of Leitão de Barros's advances in filmmaking. At the end of *A Canção de Lisboa*, the audience delights in hearing Vasco pick up a refrain from a Fado, and remembers that while *A Canção de Lisboa* is, technically-speaking, Portugal's first *filme falado* [talkie], it is the Nation's second *filme cantado* [singing picture].

The Marymount Manhattan College Sokol Award allowed me to spend three months in Lisbon, Portugal in 2008 and 2009, to use the Cinemateca Portuguesa–Museu do Cinema and the Biblioteca Nacional to write this article.

MARYMOUNT MANHATTAN COLLEGE

---

[62] Dantas, *A Severa*, p. 236.

The Aquatic Unconscious: Water Imagery in Eça de Queirós's *A Cidade e as Serras*

ESTELA VIEIRA

For centuries the sea has played a significant role in shaping Portuguese identity and culture. There has always existed a strong proximity between the element of water and the country's people, traditions, politics and socio-economic reality. Historians and cultural critics alike have long understood that the aquatic has not only factually moulded Portuguese history but also, and perhaps more importantly, has become a metaphor that has over time fascinated Portuguese writers, thinkers and artists. This creative and scientific work has been interested on the one hand in exploring the historical and cultural links between Portugal and the aquatic, and on the other hand in addressing the mythification of the sea and of the heroes of the Portuguese Discoveries, which has at different moments been used to promote politically conservative agendas.[1] According to Hans Blumenberg's *Shipwreck with Spectator* the metaphor of the sea voyage serves as a paradigm for existence.[2] This universal metaphor gains a particular profile and complexity in the Portuguese imaginary. Because the country's political greatness and colonial dominance has depended on the sea, in order to critique this hegemonic project, historians, philosophers, and even novelists, have time and again scrutinized and ironized this metaphor.

One of Portugal's most important nineteenth-century literary figures, Eça de Queirós, is a perfect example of a writer whose fiction develops a satirical discourse of the country's history of the sea. He does this nowhere else as strongly as in his late, highly humorous, and complex novel, *A Cidade e as*

---

[1] Historian Charles R. Boxer is one of the most famous chroniclers of Portugal's perils and successes on the high seas. He published a number of books on Portuguese maritime and colonial history. Another important historian of the Portuguese overseas empire, A. J. R. Russell-Wood, not only acknowledges the importance of the sea and its relation to Portuguese history, but is also careful to note that this aspect is in fact often overemphasized, and that Portuguese expansion in the Age of Discoveries can not be fully understood without also taking into account the land advances that the Portuguese made. Literary critic K. David Jackson explores in *Os Construtores dos Oceanos* (Lisbon: Assírio & Alvim, 1997) the symbolic power of the oceans in Portuguese poetic and linguistic traditions. Isabel Capeloa Gil's edited volume *Fleeting, Floating, Flowing: Water Writing and Modernity* (Würzburg: Königshausen & Neumann, 2008), which brings together a set of essays on the interactions between water writing and the construct of modernity, attests to the pertinence of the theme of water for cultural studies in general and for Portugal in particular.

[2] Hans Blumenberg, *Shipwreck with Spectator* (Cambridge, MA: MIT Press, 1997).

Serras. The author writes what we might call a tragic-comic history of the sea in this novel. His understanding of Portugal as a seafaring nation is informed by the classic eighteenth-century collection of Portuguese shipwreck narratives, *História Trágico-Marítima*, appropriating the historical and literary context of these narratives to shape his own critical and comical interpretation of the relation between the Portuguese and the sea. The major themes of the novel depend on an important topology of water, which uses the commonplace of the aquatic as representative of Portugal. Eça juxtaposes modernity with the past as he does in much of his work, but nowhere else as intensely, and uses water to mediate the conflicts between tradition and innovation by making the element of water represent both Portuguese history and modernization. As we will see the aquatic not only refers back to the country's maritime past but also relates to modern practices in plumbing and hygiene. The prolific use of water imagery in the novel is not only thematic but also formal. The first half of the story makes this point very clear. An abundance of books, ideas, luxury goods, technological inventions and modern gadgets simultaneously crowd Jacinto's mansion, life, and mind, and inundate the text with descriptive detail. Any reader of the novel would agree that the story is full of excesses that seem to drown characters and readers alike. There are real and figurative floods in the story that play a prominent role in the plot and character development. The language, the story line and the text itself are like a sea for the reader, the same way we find Jacinto on a figurative sea journey as his consciousness is caught between modernity and history. In this essay I argue that the symbolic aquatic constellation the author draws upon in his novel functions to create an awareness of depth and ambiguity that replicates not only human consciousness but also the novel's multiple levels of meaning.

Despite the significant topology of water throughout the narrative, to my knowledge no critical essay thus far studies the water imagery in a systematic way. Water as a trope has generally escaped literary criticism on this novel. For too long critical readings have tended to oversimplify the text's significance by concentrating primarily on determining if *A Cidade e as Serras* is a thesis novel. Because of the book's dualistic structure — the first half is set in Paris and the second in a small rural town in the north of Portugal — it is no surprise scholars should focus on this question. The protagonist, the wealthy and idle Jacinto, moves from his super-modernized Parisian mansion to his family's decaying ancestral home, apparently trading a hyper-civilized but empty urban existence for the simplicities of an enriching and idyllic country life. I use the word 'apparently' because, in spite of this duality, the novel makes no straightforward proposal and remains in fact one of the author's most complex and enigmatic. Furthermore, specific textual characteristics make it even more difficult to arrive at a definitive reading of *A Cidade e as Serras*. The novel was published in 1901, a year after the author's death, and Eça did not have the opportunity to review the proofs of the last chapters, leading Carlos Reis, organizer of the critical editions of Eça's complete works, to classify the novel as semi-posthumous. It is well known that the author often made substantial changes to his writings, so that it is impossible to say exactly what the final version of the last part of the novel would have looked like. Therefore even if the text were a thesis novel what it argues remains ambiguous and multiple. Perhaps it does sharply criticize the malaises of urban society and propose a return to a peaceful rural way of life. Perhaps Eça writes yet another satire about the decadent aristocracy and the turn-of-the-century dandy and their static and futile habits, whether they settle in the city or in the countryside. Perhaps, as the title *A Cidade e as Serras* suggests, the answer to our ongoing questions lies in a compromise between what innovation and tradition have to offer. Or perhaps the novel argues for the impossibility of a thesis, by giving us an ironic rendering of a thesis narrative only to reveal its misconceptions.[3] More recent scholarship, especially that of Ana Nascimento Piedade, has revisited Eça's late work and disregarded the possibility that *A Cidade e as Serras* defends a specific thesis.[4] Instead Piedade's and others' readings focus on exploring the author's complex use of ambiguity, humour, irony and myth, and argue that Eça's late writings already anticipate Portuguese modernism.[5] Some of the more recent critical interpretations begin to discuss the aquatic images but none sees the ubiquity of the *topos* as a structuring element in the novel. By looking more closely at the figure of water in *A Cidade e as Serras* we get a sense of the complexity with which Eça intended to underline his deceptively simple story, and begin to uncover some of the author's more meaningful intentions.

★ ★ ★ ★ ★

Since Antiquity water has been one of the four elements used by philosophers to explain nature. In a novel that juxtaposes nature with civilization we would expect water to be primarily associated with the natural world. Contrary to that expectation, however, water imagery is ubiquitous throughout the novel,

[3] See Frank F. Sousa's *O Segredo de Eça: Ideologia e Ambiguidade em 'A Cidade e as Serras'* (Lisbon: Cosmos, 1996), pp. 9–11 for a comprehensive synthesis of the criticism dealing with questions on *A Cidade e as Serras* as a thesis novel.

[4] See Ana Nascimento Piedade, *Ironia e Socratismo em 'A Cidade e as Serras'* (Lisbon: Instituto Camões, 2002) and her *Fradiquismo e Modernidade no Último Eça 1888–1900* (Lisbon: Imprensa Nacional–Casa da Moeda, 2003) for a thorough analysis of Eça's literary aesthetics in his late novels.

[5] See Pedro Serra's chapter on Eça de Queirós in *Filologia & Romance* (São Paulo: Nankin, 2004) for a discussion on the complexity of the library and questions of textual authority. Américo António Lindeza Diogo and Sérgio Paulo Guimarães de Sousa analyse the use of myth in *O Último Eça: O Romance e o Mito* (Braga: Irmandades da Fala da Galiza e Portugal, 2001). In *Os Caminhos do Patriarca: Representação, Tempo e Romance no 'Último Eça'* (Braga: Irmandades da Fala da Galiza e Portugal, 2001) Américo António Lindeza Diogo studies a number of topics in the novel from sexual desire to the *Odyssey*'s role in the story. Abel Barros Baptista's collected volume *'A Cidade e as Serras': Uma Revisão* (Coimbra: Angelus Novus, 2001) joins together a number of original essays with different perspectives on the novel.

present both in the French metropolis and in the Portuguese countryside. In fact one could argue it emerges more prominently in the first half of the novel, which narrates Jacinto's and Zé Fernandes's indolent existence mostly set in the former's luxurious home, number 202 on the Champs-Élysées. In touring both the French capital and his friend's Parisian house, Zé Fernandes, the first-person narrator, draws a number of comparisons that suggest that urban living is like a turbulent voyage on the open seas. We know for example that nature horrifies Jacinto and that even after a short bucolic walk in the Montmorency he quickly urges a return home. For Jacinto, coming back to the city centre is to 'mergulhar nas ondas lustrais da Civilização' (p. 21) [plunge into the purifying waves of Civilization (p. 12)].[6] After some brief background the novel's story begins with the narrator's return to Paris after an absence of seven years in his native Portugal. When he comes back, Zé Fernandes finds his friend worn-out, while Jacinto's splendid French residence on the contrary boasts a number of improvements. The narrator takes a detailed tour of number 202 which starts with a brief ride on the very handsome new elevator. This luxurious, albeit utterly superfluous, piece of transportation carries the two characters as a submarine would into what feels like the depths of the ocean. Stepping out of the elevator the narrator explains that 'Na antecâmara, onde desembarcámos' (p. 26) [In the antechamber, where we disembarked (p. 18)] the atmosphere is warm and humid and a welcoming aromatic vapour fills the air. As they enter the library overflowing with books, the narrator explains 'penetrámos numa nave cheia de majestade e sombra' (p. 26) [we entered a majestic, shadowy temple (p. 18)].[7] The intimacy of these descriptions suggests that Jacinto's personal quarters are representative of his inner world. If the aquatic opens access to the protagonist's psychic depths, it would seem that in order to penetrate inside Jacinto's private dwellings and thoughts some sea travel is necessary. From the very beginning of the novel, then, the water imagery serves to mediate between Jacinto's individual existence and the outside world.

The two characters continue their tour of the house by visiting Jacinto's study, where the narrator figuratively drowns in the intensity of the lush décor and his footsteps disappear in the thickness of the carpets. One lonely light in this silent room shines on top of a bookshelf, 'solitária como uma torre numa planície, e de que o lume parecia ser o farol melancólico' (p. 27) [solitary as a tower or a melancholy beacon in the middle of a plain (p. 19)].[8] Everything in the study is green, 'verde de mar sombrio' (p. 27) [sombre sea-green],[9] the

---

[6] José Maria Eça de Queirós, *A Cidade e as Serras* (Lisbon: Livros do Brasil, 2002). All translations come from Margaret Jull Costa's translation *The City and the Mountains* (New York: New Directions, 2008) unless otherwise noted.
[7] The word *nave* can refer to the central hall of a church, but also to a ship.
[8] The word *farol* can refer to a beacon or to a lighthouse.
[9] My translation.

damask-covered walls, the woodwork, the lampshades, the upholstery and the marble mantelpiece. Immersed and apparently lost among Jacinto's sea-like world, Zé Fernandes has a peculiar first-time encounter with his friend's many and varied sophisticated technological gadgets. Amazed, he reads a newly arrived telegraph sending word that 'a fragata russa *Azoff* entrara em Marselha com avaria' (p. 28) [the Russian frigate *Azoff* had put in at Marseilles with mechanical problems (p. 21)]. Like Jacinto's return to the city from his nature-walk, the narrator's arrival in Paris and his visit to No. 202 — in other words his introduction to the modernized world Jacinto has immersed himself in — is also compared to the challenge of penetrating uncharted seas. But apparently the characters' metaphoric voyages of discovery and conquest, as with Portugal's many historic tragic sea journeys that ended in shipwrecks, are not all a great success. Instead, just like the Russian frigate, these aquatic vessels to modernity often stall on their way. As we will see the difficult and symbolic travels through water suggest that subconscious forces determine Jacinto's fate, and that his destiny is linked to a collective past.

When Zé Fernandes asks his friend if the *Azoff* is of any concern to him, Jacinto says no. He is unaware, of course, but the frigate's engine failure is in fact detrimental to the protagonist and instrumental to the plot development. The breakdown announced on the telegraph prefigures a number of succeeding disasters, all of which are aquatic in nature and which lead up to Jacinto's final decision to make his journey to Portugal. The first takes place one Saturday night, not too long after Zé Fernandes has returned to Paris. The two experience 'um desses brutos e revoltos terrores como só os produz a ferocidade dos Elementos' (p. 44) [one of those violent and ferocious terrors that can only be produced by the wildness of the Elements (p. 39)]. Jacinto's advanced plumbing system fails when a hot water pipe bursts and begins to inundate the luxurious house with steaming water 'furiosamente, fumegando e silvando' (p. 44) [in a furious torrent, smoking and steaming (p. 40)]. The personification of water in this scene operates as a synecdoche for all of nature, which seems to be rebelling against modernization's attempts to suppress it: 'E como se todas as forças da natureza, submetidas ao serviço de Jacinto, se agitassem, animadas por aquela rebelião da água — ouvimos roncos surdos no interior das paredes, e pelos fios dos lumes eléctricos sulcaram faíscas ameaçadoras!' (p. 44) [And as if all the forces of Nature, hitherto subordinated to Jacinto's service, were rising up and taking courage from that watery rebellion, we heard dull snarls coming from inside the walls and saw threatening sparks springing from electric cables! (p. 40)]. Frank Sousa and other critics have observed how Jacinto's attempts to master nature with modern inventions are repeatedly unsuccessful and result in the opposite effect: it is the surroundings that end up controlling Jacinto and making him prisoner to his machines and obligations. As Sousa explains, water has an unconscious power: 'A Natureza possui como que uma potência inconsciente e imponente, que resiste à ciência e à razão' [Nature possesses a kind of unconscious and majestic power, which resists science and reason].[10] Water's rebellious potential here reinforces the juxtaposition in the novel between natural and human forces, but it also makes a significant political comment. The narrator's description emphasizes the sonorous qualities of the water. Critical readings on water symbolism often conclude that the aquatic in literary texts normally expresses silence. Carol Prunhuber, for example, describes in her work how water becomes the word of silence.[11] In *A Cidade e as Serras* water may have the power to silence, but more often, quite to the contrary, it speaks out with a loud voice, producing disorder and uproar. In view of the emergence of the masses in the nineteenth century as a new historical subject, the rebellious water here could also signify the power of the socially undifferentiated working classes. This not only points to Eça's liberal politics but also underpins the important social critique in the novel.[12] Interestingly Jacques Rancière argues in *The Names of History* that in the nineteenth century there is an important metaphoric displacement of history to the sea. He writes that the aquatic world accounts for 'the long periods of the life of the masses and of the dynamics of economic development'.[13] On the surface, Jacinto's flooded Parisian house seems to depict just another comical scene. Yet, by making complex historical and political connections, the imagery and the irony framing the event deliberately turn shallow waters into depth of meaning. The chaos of the water figuratively represents a social rebellion, or a subversive act, and this in turn relates to Eça's interpretation of Portugal's aquatic history. The author is suggesting that Portugal's maritime history was not only about power, but also full of tragedy and disorder that undermined the country's dominant historical narrative.

Besides making important political and historical allusions, the aquatic disaster in Jacinto's house is vital for the novel's plot development because it has the power to propel the protagonist and the story onto a different course. The water imagery in the novel continues to develop an ironic and metaphoric thread in the narrative that questions how an individual's subconscious is bound to historical experience. This becomes evident from the way other characters react to and interpret the calamity that strikes number 202. According to Jacinto, such catastrophes and floods have happened before and are a sign of nothing but the impotent modern plumbing industry. On the other hand, all

[10] Sousa, p. 27.

[11] In *Agua, Silencio, Memoria y Felisberto Hernandez* (Caracas: Academia Nacional de la Historia, 1986), Carol Prunhuber studies water as a poetic figure in the work of Hernandez arguing that it represents 'el mundo insonoro pleno de silencio' [the soundless world, full of silence] (p. 184).

[12] In the afterword to her translation Margaret Jull Costa claims that it is the novel's social commentary and its ability to portray social struggle and the 'divide between the haves and the have-nots' that makes Eça's story especially relevant to today's reader (p. 282).

[13] Jacques Rancière, *The Names of History*, trans. by Hassan Melehy (Minneapolis: University of Minnesota Press, 1994), p. 12.

of Paris, including *Figaro*, construes the event as a natural disaster. It seems contradictory that a natural disaster should occur as a result of technological advancements, and in the heart of a modern cosmopolitan capital at that. Jacinto's acquaintances, Parisian high society, make revealing comments that are highly humorous, but also, and more importantly, connect the event specifically to the protagonist. Grand Duke Casimiro sends an urgent telegram: 'O quê! O meu Jacinto inundado! Muito chique, nos Campos Elísios! Não volto ao 202 sem bóia de salvação!' (p. 45) ['What! My Jacinto flooded out! Very chic and in the Champs-Élysées too! The next time I visit No. 202 I'll bring a life buoy! Condolences, Casimiro' (p. 42)]. Madame d'Oriol rushes over, dying of curiosity to admire the ruins: 'não me contive, quis ver os estragos... Uma inundação em Paris, nos Campos Elísios! Não há senão este Jacinto' (p. 47) ['I couldn't help myself, I simply had to see the damage. A flood in Paris, in the Champs-Élysées! Such a thing could only happen to Jacinto' (p. 43)]. Jacinto is seen as unable to navigate the urban sphere since the disaster pins his personal failure at being ultramodern upon the city of Paris as a whole. In other words the result of Jacinto's pioneering spirit ultimately brings a natural disaster to the centre of modernity. There are various levels of irony here which contribute to Eça's critique of both Jacinto and France, and of what the country symbolizes, as Beatriz Berrini explains: 'a França metonimicamente representa as nações dominadoras do mundo' [France represents metonymically the dominant nations of the world].[14] The natural disaster once at odds with the rationalized world represents also the return of myth to modernity and therefore harks back to Jacinto's Portuguese roots.[15] There is no recognition that this event indicates the failure of the French modern plumbing system but instead it is seen as a result of a Portuguese inheritance. The flood brings to the forefront national traditions along with personal memories. Casimiro and Madame d'Oriol's light-hearted comments to Jacinto affect him in a profound way because they tap unconscious processes both individual and collective. Aquatic events in the novel begin to move Jacinto in the direction of Portugal and relate the protagonist's subconscious to his historical tradition. The return home, *nostos*,

---

[14] Beatriz Berrini, 'Jacinto aristocrata rural', *Colóquio–Letras*, 97 (May/June 1987), pp. 26–36 (p. 29).

[15] Américo António Lindeza Diogo and Sérgio Paulo Guimarães de Sousa study the mythical references in the novel, as mentioned earlier, and focus on some of the aquatic elements. They read in Jacinto's characterization different myths of origin in relation to the river metaphor that Zé Fernandes uses to describe his friend's birth. The continuous rain that pervades the novel they interpret, like other critics, as emblematic of Jacinto once in Portugal having traded one existence for another: 'O Jacinto das serras, que recuperou condições de vida primordiais, é um homem pós-diluvial' [The Jacinto of the mountains, who has salvaged the primordial conditions of life, is a postdiluvian man] (*O Último Eça: O Romance e o Mito*, p. 140). I hope to show that, in fact, the rains and aquatic metaphors continue in Tormes, so that while the city, or civilization, figuratively drown Jacinto, fleeing to the mountains will not save him from sinking but instead confront him with a collective consciousness.

is of course the basic narrative structure of the *Odyssey*, a crucial inter-text and literary tradition informing the novel. As with Jacinto, the aquatic metaphors also act as a formal influence on the author himself. Eça looks to both return to and depart from literary traditions as he narrates modernity's contradictions and conflicts.

The sequence of catastrophes continues when this unexpected inundation is followed by another uncommon disaster. Jacinto gives an elaborate dinner party in honour of the Grand Duke Casimiro, who has brought a rare and exotic Dalmatian fish for the occasion. The previous time in the novel when a fish was ordered and especially prepared for someone there were devastating results, as Jacinto 'Galeão', the protagonist's grandfather, had died of indigestion from 'uma lampreia de escabeche' (p. 13) [a dish of pickled lamprey (p. 4)], which he had shipped back from Portugal. As we will see, the connection to Jacinto's forefather reinforces the narrative logic that the aquatic events follow in the novel. The narrator tells the reader that practically all of the dominant social classes of France seem to be sitting at Jacinto's elaborate dinner table. The disaster, which is also the final climactic event of the evening, begins when the dumb waiter gets stuck on its way up to serve the much-awaited baked fish. The entire dinner party anxiously gathers around the dark well of the lift to admire their unreachable main course: 'O grão-duque lá estava, debruçado sobre o poço escuro do elevador, onde mergulhara uma vela que lhe avermelhava mais a face esbraseada' (p. 66) [The Grand Duke was already there, peering into the black well of the lift and holding a candle that made his flushed face seem still redder (p. 67)]. The narrator also peeks below and observes: 'Em baixo, na treva, sobre uma larga prancha, o peixe precioso alvejava, deitado na travessa, ainda fumegando, entre rodelas de limão' (p. 66) [Down below, in the darkness, on a large platter, surrounded by slices of lemon, lay the precious fish, white and gleaming, the steam still rising from it (p. 67)].[16] Madame de Todelle has the brilliant idea to fish the fish from the dumb waiter. Everyone but Jacinto seems to think this an excellent solution and they all enthusiastically cheer the Grand Duke along as he attempts unsuccessfully to rescue the appetizing fish from the depths. Jacinto suffers throughout this comic tragedy and patiently limits himself to illuminating the lift-shaft in an attempt to help the Duke.

The fishing, even if unsuccessful, lightens the mood and everyone's spirits, and as the rest of the party returns to the dinner table Madame de Trèves stays behind to tell Jacinto how much she admires his pantry, including the dumb waiter. She says to him: 'Oh, perfeita! Que compreensão da vida, que fina inteligência do conforto!' (p. 68) [It was perfect! What an acute understanding of life it revealed, what a keen appreciation of comfort! (p. 69)]. Her comment makes it clear that the dumb waiter is representative of Jacinto's view of the

---

[16] More than 'platter', *prancha* suggests any of its many aquatic meanings; a gangplank, a floating wooden board, a stage on the side of a ship, a surfboard.

world. The dark hole gives access to Jacinto's inner mind and subconscious thoughts. The fish stuck beneath evokes the fatal fish that killed his grandfather and also allows the entire dinner party, all of the dominant Parisian social classes, to interrogate, mock, and ultimately abandon Jacinto's deeper self. Like the bursting hot-water pipes, the stalled fish once again juxtaposes the aquatic to the technological, and creates a parallel between Jacinto's unconscious world and his and his native country's past. Jacinto's failed attempts to be hyper-modern are like Portugal's historically curtailed pioneering maritime ambitions. Soon after this event Jacinto receives some important news from Portugal that will forever change the course of events in the novel. The letter that arrives from Tormes is clearly the climactic moment that the narrative has been working up to with these previous aquatic traumas. This sequence of events interrupts the course of modern life and opens in this disruption the space for conflict between modernization and tradition, and between Jacinto and his past. It is no surprise therefore that the climax should also be brought on by an abundance of water. Nor that exactly three days after the dinner party the novel introduces the third and last water incident that repeats and closes this aquatic cycle of disasters.

> Três dias depois desta festa no 202 recebeu o meu Príncipe inesperadamente, de Portugal, uma nova considerável. Sobre a sua quinta e solar de Tormes, por toda a serra, passara uma tormenta devastadora de vento, corisco e água. Com as grossas chuvas, 'ou por outras causas que os peritos dirão' (como exclamava na sua carta angustiada o procurador Silvério), um pedaço de monte, que se avançava em socalcos sobre o vale da Carriça, desabara, arrastando a velha igreja, uma igrejinha rústica do século XVI, onde jaziam sepultados os avós de Jacinto desde os tempos de el-rei D. Manuel. (pp. 69–70)

> [Three days after the party at No. 202, my Prince unexpectedly received some important news from Portugal. A devastating storm of wind, lightning and rain had struck his house and estate in Tormes and, indeed, the whole area. With the heavy rain, 'or for some other reason that the experts have yet to reveal' (in the words of his evidently distraught administrator, Silvério), a section of the hillside that overhung the Vale da Carriça had collapsed, dragging with it the old church — a little rustic chapel built in the sixteenth century, and in which Jacinto's male forebears had had their final resting-place ever since the days of King Manuel.] (pp. 71–72)

A terrible rainstorm causes Jacinto's ancestors to figuratively rise from the dead. Another wet disaster rushes forward to interrupt and disturb Jacinto's consciousness. Once again Eça's ironic treatment imagines an inundation that unearths instead of covering up or drowning, as one would expect. The aquatic events function then to probe Jacinto's unconscious thoughts and anxieties and the conflicting traditions of Portugal's past.

We can easily tie these defining incidents in the plot to Jacinto's psyche because his characterization depends heavily on a fascination with water.

According to Zé Fernandes, Jacinto is the proud owner of an infamous collection of every kind of water imaginable: 'Todo um aparador porém vergava sob o luxo redundante, quase assustador de águas — águas oxigenadas, águas carbonatadas, águas fosfatadas, águas esterilizadas, águas de sais, outras ainda, em garrafas bojudas, com tratados terapêuticos impressos em rótulos' (p. 34) [The whole of one dresser, though, groaned beneath an entirely unnecessary and almost frightening array of bottled waters — oxygenated water, carbonated water, phosphated water, sterilized water, soda water, as well as others in pot-bellied bottles with therapeutic treatises printed on the labels (pp. 27–28)]. Upon his return from Portugal the narrator reminds readers that Jacinto is still 'o mesmo tremendo bebedor de água... *Un aquatico!*' (p. 34) [still a great drinker of water! An "aquatic"! (p. 28)]. Despite this great wealth of choices Jacinto complains he has yet to find a type of water that satisfies him, in fact he says 'Até sofro sede' (p. 34) ['I sometimes go thirsty' (p. 28)], like D. Angelina Fafes, his grandmother, who decides to continue living in Paris after her husband's death in spite of terribly missing the good water of Alcolena (p. 13). In Jacinto's mansion the 'Sala de Banho' [bathroom] is 'a mais extremada maravilha do 202' (p. 37) [No. 202's greatest marvel (p. 31)]. The narrator is at once fascinated and frightened by the modernized plumbing, which includes different hot water faucets for Jacinto's body, head, teeth, and shaving needs. His physical and psychological self is bound to a need of water that comes from a lack. The narrator describes the bathroom as a 'recanto temeroso, onde delgados tubos mantinham em disciplina e servidão tantas águas ferventes, tantas águas violentas' (p. 37) [dread place — in which all that violent, boiling water was kept disciplined and enslaved in some alarmingly slender pipes (p. 31)]. Water is again portrayed as a rebellious, subversive element, which the protagonist attempts to dominate or repress. Jacinto apparently overcompensates for his hollow and arid sense of existence with these different obsessions and attempts to control water. The protagonist's fixation with liquids recalls what Sigmund Freud termed as an obsessive–compulsive disorder typical of neurotic behaviour. If we read this as Jacinto following in his grandmother's footsteps, and living out her trauma, then it would seem that the protagonist's current psychic condition is informed by his forefathers' experiences. Instead of functioning, as it traditionally does in literary texts, as a representation of a character's narcissistic self-reflection, the aquatic obsessions in Eça's novel point to a deeper knowledge of events and encounters. Jacinto's physical longing for water, his thirst, inscribes him in a tradition and repeats a family trauma that is also national. Transgenerational trauma is used here as a model for history.

The narrative builds on these different aquatic events and on Jacinto's fascination with water in the first half of the story to prepare the characters' trip across the Iberian Peninsula. The journey that Jacinto and Zé Fernandes make entails labouring across mountainous terrain but ironically it resembles even more a sea voyage. In fact the protagonist seems to have already embarked on an aquatic adventure even before he has left Paris. This becomes evident during an important scene where Jacinto shares his anxieties with the narrator about the travelling. As a guest in Jacinto's Parisian home, Zé Fernandes occupies Galeão's former sleeping quarters. It is in this room that Jacinto announces his wish to go to Tormes and discusses the reasons for his decision. Jacinto's wanderings about the bedroom indicate his great sense of uncertainty: 'vagou pelo quarto, topando nas cadeiras, embicando contra os postes torneados do velho leito de 'D. Galeão', num balanço vago, como barco já desamarrado do seu seguro ancoradouro, e sem rumo no mar incerto' (p. 115) [wandered about the room, bumping into chairs, colliding with the posts on Dom Galeão's ancient bed, and rocking slightly, like a boat untied from its safe mooring and setting off with no fixed course across an uncertain sea (p. 125)]. The physical proximity of Jacinto to his grandfather's bed relates the ambiguity and torment he is presently experiencing to the various wanderings of his forefathers. It ironically refers both to Galeão's exile to France and to Portugal's seafaring ventures; both movements provoked by historical contexts marked by the conflict between modernity and tradition. This sea-journey metaphor is intensified by other details of the trip. Determined to leave despite his fears, Jacinto prepares himself for the voyage by stocking up on every type of water he might deem necessary for his comfort, and the ride through Spain is anything but tranquil and, unsurprisingly, plagued by torrential rains. The train runs terribly late making the two characters almost miss their connection in Medina. In order to catch their second train, Zé Fernandes and Jacinto are forced by the wild storm outside to face the downpour, run through puddles, fight the wind and water, and leave all their belongings behind. Arriving in Portugal with none of their possessions, only to discover that no one awaits them, the two sit on a bench at the station, weary, defeated, 'como náufragos' (p. 134) [as shipwreck victims (p. 148)].[17] The trip therefore puts Jacinto through yet another aquatic test, flooding him once again in order to wash away and purge him of the material possessions that tied him to his life in Paris. The Spanish rainstorm connects to the previous inundations in the story, the 202 flood and the rains in Tormes. Similarly, the stormy voyage paradoxically uncovers latent psyche

---

[17] In Abel Barros Baptista's organized volume 'A Cidade e as Serras': Uma Revisão, Roberto Vecchi's essay 'Naufrágio à Portuguesa' juxtaposes Eça's novel with Daniel Defoe's Robinson Crusoe and it reads the significance between modernity and experience. He points to Eça's rendering of Jacinto as a shipwreck victim: 'Jacinto naufraga naquele mar que é a civilização moderna; a modernidade, com efeito, como o mar, transforma-se na esfera do imprevisível, do caos, do desnorteamento; como o naufrágio ' [Jacinto is shipwrecked on the sea of modern civilization; in effect, modernity, like the sea, is transformed into the sphere of the unpredictable, of chaos, of disorientation; like a shipwreck] (p. 83). As other critics, Vecchi sees the aquatic metaphors as representing the city, and that in Tormes, Jacinto has escaped the threatening sea. I, on the other hand, argue that aquatic metaphors have a deeper meaning in the novel that is not only related to Jacinto abandoning the city for the mountains.

encounters that bring Jacinto closer to his Portuguese identity. The excess of water allows for the necessary repetition of both individual and collective past experiences.

It is easy to connect this Iberian sea journey to Jacinto's inner self because of the way the narrator describes their transition into Portugal. Before the two arrive at their final destination, exhausted by their taxing trip, they fall into a deep sleep. As the train crosses the border into Portugal, Zé Fernandes wakes up to admire the idyllic surroundings while Jacinto remains asleep. The narrator is obliged to arouse Jacinto and insist that he contemplate the beautiful landscape and pay particular attention to the river Douro, whose margin the train follows. The river emerges as a central metaphor at the very moment of transition into Portugal. This is especially important because at the beginning of the novel the narrator uses the river as an archetype for Jacinto's life when he refers ironically to the privileged existence of his 'Príncipe da Grã-Ventura' (p. 16).[18] The train and the river running parallel convey an image that emblematically brings the city and the mountains, nature and civilization, closer together. The novel's crucial thematic concern, the juxtaposition of modernity and tradition, so embedded in the text's structure, emerges at this significant moment of reflection and transition. Even more crucial is the fact that Jacinto sleeps his way into Portugal. It suggests that his new life in Tormes is closely connected to his dream world and insinuates that Jacinto never confronts spaces of conflict but instead suffers passively the contradictions between modernity and tradition, his past and present existence, and his conscious and unconscious worlds. The parallel further implies that subconscious energies flow similarly to rivers and trains, not only generating the progress of the narrative but also giving shape to the novel's thematic conflicts. As Gaston Bachelard has shown in his famous phenomenological study, *Water and Dreams*, water's revealing qualities, its depth, receptiveness, liquidity, and reflective power, explain why water imagery populates our dreams and reveries and becomes the matter of the imagination.[19] Eça's novel connects the aquatic with the dream world and explores how water imagery influences the development of narrative. But the author is further interested in what links imagination, or fiction, with historiography and therefore his story is also concerned with tying human consciousness to social experience, and he does this by creating an ironic and critical connection between a collective past and a personal identity.

Once he settles in at his family estate in Portugal, Jacinto's fondness of water

---

[18] Another example that reveals the ironic association between the river and Jacinto takes place at Zé Fernandes's birthday party celebration when one of his guests, Rojão, reminds Jacinto that he owns 'uma larga faixa do Douro, com privilégio para a pesca do sável' (p. 212) [a long stretch of the Douro and had the right to fish for shad in it (p. 236)]. Unfortunately the river as a metaphor for a full and fruitful life is not what it seems, for there are no shad left in the Douro.

[19] Gaston Bachelard, *Water and Dreams: An Essay on the Imagination of Matter*, trans. by Edith R. Farrell (Dallas: Pegasus Foundation, 1983).

will change in nature but not in intensity. To the surprise of the readers Jacinto is now perfectly satisfied to use for his toilette only the lavender water that the narrator sends to him from Guiães and has abandoned the endless varieties of water he used in Paris. When Zé Fernandes returns to Tormes for the first time after parting with his friend, he first observes the rooms of the house just as at the beginning of the novel he toured No. 202. Before meeting with Jacinto, Zé Fernandes penetrates the protagonist's private interior spaces and discovers order in the rooms, and the floor 'borrifado de água' (p. 154) [freshly sprinkled with water (p. 171)], which further enhances the morning's freshness and splendid stillness. Zé Fernandes takes a volume from Jacinto's bookshelves and playfully adapts two verses from Virgil, which reinforce the narrator's idea that his friend might finally find peace and happiness in the natural beauty of Tormes: 'Afortunado Jacinto, na verdade! Agora, entre campos que são teus e águas que te são sagradas, colhes enfim a sombra e a paz!' (p. 154) ['Fortunate Jacinto indeed! Now amid these fields which are yours and these waters that are sacred to you, you can enjoy at last your harvest of shade and peace!' (p. 172)].[20] Once Jacinto comes in to greet the narrator he tells him that he is no longer thirsty and loves the many and endless springs his estate provides. He also assures Zé Fernandes he will remain in Tormes for as long as the 'água da fonte' (p. 155) [the water from the fountain (p. 173)] continues to taste divinely to him, and announces to his friend with enthusiasm: 'Pesquei já hoje quatro trutas' (p. 155) ['Today I caught four magnificent trout' (p. 173)]. Zé Fernandes asks 'Oh Jacinto! E as águas carbonatadas? e as fosfatadas? e as esterilizadas? e as sódicas?...' (p. 157) ['Jacinto! What about the carbonated water and the phosphated water and the sterilized water and the soda water?' (p. 175)], and Jacinto proudly shrugs his shoulders. Although Jacinto has apparently made changes to some of his obsessions, the abundance of water remains a theme throughout the rest of the story and Jacinto is in fact no less aquatic. When Jacinto comes up with the grand idea of building a goat-cheese factory on his estate, Zé Fernandes tells him: 'Sim... Trazes a água para o prado. Águas não faltam na serra' (p. 173) ['Yes. You could bring the water down to the meadow, and there's no shortage of water in the mountains' (p. 193)]. In this mountainous

[20] Virgil is not the only important reference Eça makes to the classics and their aquatic metaphors. The *Odyssey* is one of the books Jacinto rediscovers and is finally able to read with pleasure during his first weeks in Tormes. He has left behind his thousands of volumes of books that did not allow him to read and the feeling of finally being able to read again is described with enthusiasm: 'Aquele grande mar da *Odisseia* — resplandecente e sonoro, sempre azul, todo azul, sob o voo branco das gaivotas' (p. 179) [The great sea of *The Odyssey* — resplendent and loud, always blue, utterly blue, beneath the white flight of the seagulls (p. 201)]. This poetic aquatic description is not only a positive description of Jacinto's good feelings but also a reference to the subconscious literary tradition and sea of imagination that inform Eça's own narrative. The *Odyssey* is a crucial inter-text, as is *Don Quixote*. *A Cidade e as Serras* can be read within the framework of Cervantes and Homer, as a double journey through Iberia and the Greek islands, and an epic comedy with heroes and anti-heroes.

natural landscape, as in the hyper-civilized urban space of Paris, a vast array of forms of water play an important role in the text. While in Tormes the narrator makes continuous references to the natural springs, the river Douro, brooks, streams, lakes, plenty of drinking water, and water inside the house and outside in the fields. Even if the variety of water in Tormes is not often trapped in pipes and bottles as it is in Paris, it becomes clear that there is always the possibility of bringing it under human or technological control. Clear evidence of this is the fact that Jacinto wishes and makes future plans to update plumbing and build factories that would use energy generated by water on his proprieties.

The abundance of water is a continuity of ironic play in both parts of the novel. The theme of rain, for example, already prevalent in the city persists in the mountains. We have seen that torrential rains and flooding are the catalyst for Jacinto's move to Portugal and a strong rainstorm underscores his strenuous journey through Spain. Rainy and grey days also characterize the ongoing sombreness of the French capital. At the beginning of the novel Zé Fernandes learns he must return to his hometown of Guiães on a grey, chilly, rainy February morning. He returns to Paris seven years later, again on a grey, chilly, late-February afternoon. It is true that it often rains in Eça's narrative worlds, but in keeping with its aquatic narrative logic things are particularly wet and muddy in *A Cidade e as Serras*. In the mountains, Zé Fernandes's birthday party, which clearly parallels, or repeats, Jacinto's dinner party in Paris, is equally interrupted by a wet disaster. The party comes to an abrupt end when a terrible thunderstorm forces the guests to return home early. These repetitions show that the aquatic is not merely a symbolic motif but a structuring element in the text as it closes circles and proves that things are not all that different in Tormes. Silvério, the manager of the estate, tries to appeal to Jacinto's deepest unconscious fears and warns him not to remain in Tormes because of the severe winter weather, the morning fog, the harsh cold, the wild winds, 'e chuvas e chuvas que se desfaz a serra!' (p. 176) ['and rain and more rain causing landslides and mudslides' (p. 197)]. The continuity of water between the city and the mountains, and a number of important scenes and situations that replicate previous events in Paris, contradicts the readings of the novel that claim the story suggests a radical transformation in Jacinto's character. The continuities far outweigh the differences between the two parts of the story. The idea of repetition is crucial for the author's topology of water because Eça's aquatic constructs tie Jacinto's characterization and the plot development to the fact that a conflicting past and shifting identities surface as unconscious recurrences of collective events. If anything the difference in the water imagery between the first and second half of the novel is more telling of Jacinto's geographical change than his psychological transition. Jacinto encounters episodes that articulate a conflict he is unable to understand but experiences nonetheless. These aquatic events do not lead to a gain in knowledge but seem to have a passive influence over the characters. Whether his muddy unconscious world has any impact on his sense of self is left ambiguous. That the novel writes an aquatic narrative of ironic critique and symbolic commentary is as clear as the sparkling spring waters of Tormes.

★ ★ ★ ★ ★

Water has a long symbolic history in literary and cultural studies. Instead of focusing on traditional representations of water, I have tried to show how Eça chooses to tie aquatic metaphors to character and plot development, seeking to uncover historical and social contexts whose forces influenced his milieu. Psychoanalysis has analysed extensively the representation of water in dreams and this has led phenomenologists and other cultural and literary theorists to explore how water is an archetype for the imagination. Carl Jung has claimed that human psyches were genuinely linked together in some way both subtle and profound and called this shared body of knowledge and connection the collective unconscious. Jacinto's aquatic obsessions that both reveal and conceal personal anxieties and uncertainties can be read as suggestive of the Portuguese collective unconscious that Eça chooses to ironically make part of his novel. Josiah Blackmore argues convincingly in *Manifest Perdition* that the shipwreck narrative tradition accounting for the calamity that many merchant Portuguese ships underwent in the sixteenth and seventeenth centuries has an unsettling and disruptive agenda, undermining the establishment of empire.[21] Eça's interpretation of Portugal's maritime history has the same effect as the earlier shipwreck narratives. Far from being what some critics have called a retrograde and reactionary novel because of its nostalgic idealization of the Portuguese countryside, *A Cidade e as Serras* is a complex, ironic and humorous story that through its subtle water imagery develops a significant critique of Portugal's maritime heroes and failed expansionist ambitions. In his reading of modernity Eça is also critically rereading an important Portuguese tradition. Modernity is not interpreted as breaking with history, but instead genealogy, unconsciousness, history and plot converge in the aquatic imagery that forms the topology of the novel and articulates the relation between modern times and the past.

INDIANA UNIVERSITY BLOOMINGTON

---

[21] Josiah Blackmore, *Manifest Perdition: Shipwreck, Narrative, and the Disruption of Empire* (Minneapolis: University of Minnesota Press, 2002).

Zola in Rio de Janeiro: The Production of Space in Aluísio Azevedo's O Cortiço

Lúcia Sá

The most frequently quoted passages from Aluísio Azevedo's 1890 Naturalist novel O Cortiço (The Slum, 1890) are those in which the narrator contrasts the lush, sensual, and dangerous American tropics with the still and melancholy Portugal, as in the following description from the point of view of the Portuguese immigrant, Piedade:

> Sim, lá os campos eram frios e melancólicos, de um verde alourado e quieto, e não ardentes e esmeraldinos e afogados em tanto sol e em tanto perfume como o deste inferno, onde em cada folha que se pisa há debaixo um réptil venenoso, como em cada flor que desabotoa e em cada moscardo que adeja há um vírus de lascívia. Lá nos saudosos campos de sua terra, não se ouviam em noites de lua clara roncar a onça e o maracajá, nem pela manhã, ao romper do dia rilhava o bando truculento das queixadas; lá não varava pelas florestas a anta feia e terrível, quebrando árvores. Lá a cascavel não chocalhava a sua campainha fúnebre, anunciando a morte, nem a coral esperava traidora o viajante descuidado para lhe dar o bote certeiro e decisivo. (p. 176)[1]

> [Yes, back in Portugal the fields were cool and melancholy, brownish-green and still, not ardent and emerald, bathed in brilliant light and perfume as in Brazil. That inferno where every blade of grass conceals some venomous reptile, where every budding flower and every buzzing bluebottle fly bears a lascivious virus. There, amidst Portugal's wistful landscapes, one didn't hear jaguars and wildcats snarling on moonlit nights, or herds of peccaries foraging at daybreak. There the hideous and dreadful tapir did not crash through forests, snapping trees; there the anaconda didn't shake its deadly rattles nor did the coral snake lie in wait for the unsuspecting traveler, ready to strike and kill.] (p. 155)[2]

Such descriptions are, however, relatively rare in the novel, perhaps because O Cortiço takes place not in a jungle full of *maracajás*, jaguars, and tapirs, but in a tenement or slum in Rio de Janeiro, where such animals are nowhere to be seen. The reason why passages like this are so often quoted has to do with the

---

[1] Aluísio Azevedo, O Cortiço [1890] (São Paulo: Círculo do Livro, 1973). All Portuguese quotations from this novel are from this edition. Page numbers are given in the text.

[2] All English translations from O Cortiço are taken from The Slum, trans. by David H. Rosenthal (New York: Oxford University Press, 1999). Page numbers are shown in the text after each quotation.

ease with which they seem to illustrate Aluísio Azevedo's adherence to Emile Zola's Naturalist thesis that humans are a product of their environment. Thus, the Portuguese immigrant Jerônimo, Piedade's husband, is described as going through profound changes after his arrival in Brazil:

> Uma transformação, lenta e profunda, operava-se nele, dia a dia, hora a hora, revscerando-lhe o corpo e alando-lhe os sentidos, num trabalho misterioso e surdo de crisálida. A sua energia afrouxava lentamente: fazia-se contemplativo e amoroso. A vida americana e a natureza do Brasil patenteavam-lhe agora aspectos imprevistos e sedutores que o comoviam; esquecia-se dos seus primitivos sonhos de ambição, para idealizar felicidades novas, picantes e violentas; tornava-se liberal, imprevidente e franco, mais amigo de gastar que de guardar; adquiria desejos, tomava gosto aos prazeres, e volvia-se preguiçoso resignando-se, vencido, às imposições do sol e do calor, muralha de fogo com que o espírito eternamente revoltado do último tambor entricheirou a pátria contra os conquistadores aventureiros. (p. 92)

> [Day by day, hour by hour, a slow but profound change was transforming him, altering his body and sharpening his senses as silently and mysteriously as a butterfly growing in its cocoon. His energy drained away, he became contemplative and easygoing. He found life in the Americas and Brazil's landscapes exciting and seductive; he forgot his earlier ambitions and began to enjoy new, pungent, strong sensations. He was more generous and less concerned about tomorrow, quicker to spend than to save. He developed desires, enjoyed his pleasures, and grew lazy, bowing in defeat before the blazing sun and hot weather: a wall of fire behind which the last Tamoio Indian's rebellious spirit defends its fatherland against conquering adventurers from overseas.] (p. 75)

It is as though Azevedo, with recourse to Romantic cliché, had to bring another type of landscape into his urban novel in order to offer his own formulaic variation on Zola's claim that the environment determines the fate of the individuals. It is true that other characters in the novel also support this deterministic thesis: the fair and gentle Pombinha, for example, in spite of her marriage to a good man, becomes a prostitute. But neither Jerônimo's nor Pombinha's transformations tell us, so to speak, the whole story. *O Cortiço* can also be read as an illustration of the opposite thesis, that is, of how — and why — human beings transform the environments around them.

This article will analyse spatial relations and practices in *O Cortiço* in order to demonstrate the novel's strong social-political critique of nineteenth-century Brazil. Critics have been for the most part reluctant to accept that Azevedo was attempting to make clear political claims through his novels. His fate has not been, in this sense, very different from that of his French model, Emile Zola. Marxist criticism has been especially remarkable for its outright rejection of Naturalism's negative analyses of capitalism. David Baguley's comment on George Lukács's essay 'The Zola Centenary' summarizes their views:

> The essay is valuable, however, less for its topicality than for the way in which it articulates an already firmly established and seemingly self-

perpetuating set of arguments against Zola and Naturalism by Marxist critics, a tradition that can be traced back to Plekhanov, Gorki, and Lafargue, and even the famous letter of Engels to Miss Harkness (of April 1888), in which Balzac is appraised as infinitely greater then 'all the Zolas past, present and future'. The recurring charges are that Zola's Naturalism is a debased form of the great Realist tradition, represented in France by Balzac; that it mechanistically assimilates society to a biological model and passes over its inherent contradictions; that except perhaps in *Germinal*, it fails to depict the class struggle and offers instead a Darwinian vision of competing social species; that it espouses a fatalistic and static worldview; that it is excessively preoccupied with peripheral detail, facts, description, documentation, failing to represent characters who convey social, as opposed to physiological or pathological significance.[3]

Brazilian critics of the time and thereafter were almost unanimous in seeing local Naturalist novels as too close to Zola's works, and therefore equally incapable of depicting local reality. Thus, contemporary reviews of Brazilian Naturalist novels often criticized their 'mau gosto' [bad taste]: the excessively open treatment of sexual behaviour; the reduction of humans to their physiological aspects; the concentration on debased aspects of life, such as diseases and pathological behaviours; their fatalism, and their outdated scientism.[4] Later critics, on the other hand, tended to repeat what Baguley called the 'already firmly established and seemingly self-perpetuating set of arguments against Zola and Naturalism by Marxist critics' (as above). Nelson Werneck Sodré, for instance, after accusing Zola of concentrating on 'aspectos exteriores da vida das classes trabalhadoras' [some external aspects of the life of the working classes],[5] describes Brazilian Naturalism as having, in comparison to the French version, 'o mesmo materialismo vulgar, o mesmo misticismo fisiológico, a mesma estreiteza artística, a mesma representação detalhista dos ambientes, o mesmo pedantismo científico do evolucionismo, do positivismo, a mesma fascinação pela histeria feminina e pelas manifestações patológicas em geral e, no fim de contas, a mesma inverossimilhança' [the same vulgar materialism, the same artistic narrowness, the same pedantic scientism of evolutionism and determinism, the same fascination with feminine hysteria and for pathological manifestations in general, and, in the end, the same inverisimilitude].[6] At the same time, he argues, since Brazilian social reality was different from that of Europe, Brazilian Naturalist novels 'are the falser the harder they try to copy

---

[3] *Critical Essays on Emile Zola*, ed. by David Baguley (Boston: G. K. Hall, 1986), p. 13.
[4] See for instance Sílvio Romero's 'Movimento Espiritual do Brasil', which, in a review of several Brazilian Naturalist novels, refers to the 'narrow-minded and sterile naturalism of Zola's school'. 'O Movimento Espiritual no Brasil', in *Sílvio Romero: Teoria, Crítica e História Literária*, ed. by Antonio Candido (São Paulo: Edusp, 1978), p. 115.
[5] Nelson Werneck Sodré, *O Naturalismo no Brasil* (Rio de Janeiro: Civilização Brasileira, 1965), p. 31.
[6] Ibid, p. 232.

the foreign recipe'.⁷ Lúcia Miguel-Pereira in *Prosa de Ficção* (1950) accused Brazilian Naturalists of dealing with 'casos de alcova' [bedroom affairs], while refusing to engage in serious analysis of a society where 'se processavam experiências raciais da maior importância, onde as relações de senhores e escravos suscitavam um sem-número de problemas' [extremely important racial experiences were being processed, and where the relationship between masters and slaves generated numerous problems].⁸

After asking why Brazilian writers tended to prefer Zola as a model to Flaubert, and Comte and Spencer to Marx, Flora Süssekind answers her own question by claiming that the 'bedroom affairs' of Brazilian Naturalism provided conservative (and comfortable) substitutes for the social problems that the writers were aware of, but preferred not to discuss.⁹ In other words, instead of approaching the conflicts that split the country around the abolition of slavery or the movements towards a Republic, writers preferred to dwell on the image of deranged women, who become a favoured metaphor for a sick society. The solution they presented for such sickness was, in turn, as conservative as possible: marriage, i.e., the straitjacket of legally constituted families in a patriarchal society.

Excellent as it is, Süssekind's analysis leaves out *O Cortiço*, which is generally considered to be the most important novel of Brazilian Naturalism. For Azevedo's novel does not fit the 'bedroom' model, as it discusses social relations between different classes, and even slavery and abolition. It is not Azevedo's depiction of social conflict, however, that receives most praise from critics: the overwhelming majority of them list as the most definitive quality of the novel its capacity to portray the movement of the crowds and collective forces — a quality also attributed to Zola by more than one of his contemporaries.¹⁰ Naomi Schor, in her book *Zola's Crowds* (1978), points out that before structuralism it was impossible to make a serious study of crowds in Zola because virtually all critics until then assumed that 'Zola (over-)compensated for his congenital ineptitude at creating "well-rounded" protagonists by creating impressive crowds'.¹¹ The same assumption surrounds most critical comments about Azevedo's crowds. Lúcia Miguel-Pereira, who considers *O Cortiço* Azevedo's masterpiece, says that the best thing about is its 'visão panorâmica' [panoramic vision] (an expression also used to refer to Zola's writings), and its capacity to show the 'espetáculo das massas' [spectacle of the masses] — a very fortunate

---

⁷ Ibid, p. 233.
⁸ Lúcia Miguel-Pereira, *Prosa de Ficção (de 1870 a 1920)* (Rio de Janeiro: José Olympio, 1950), p. 126.
⁹ Flora Süssekind, *Tal Brasil, Qual Romance? Uma Ideologia Estética e sua História: Naturalismo* (Rio de Janeiro: Achiamé, 1984), p. 53.
¹⁰ Jules Lamaître lauded Zola's ability to depict collective forces, and Emile Faguet, after giving a very negative vew of Zola's works, conceded that he had a 'special talent for depicting the crowds' (quoted in English in Baguley's *Critical Essays*, p. 5).
¹¹ Naomi Schor, *Zola's Crowds* (Baltimore, MD: Johns Hopkins University Press, 1978), p. xiii.

phrase that is then repeated by practically every critic afterwards. Echoing the phenomenon described by Schor, she adds that 'Só nos momentos em que vê o indivíduo em função do meio a que pertence, como parte dele, e não como um caso a estudar isoladamente, é que o escritor se sente no seu elemento' [The writer feels within his own element only in those moments when he sees the individual as a function of the environment, as part of it, and not as a case to be studied in isolation].[12] Álvaro Lins rehearses the same argument, claiming that Azevedo 'Nunca pôde manter uma atitude psicológica em face do homem isolado, mas soube, com uma eficiência surpreendente, penetrar no interior dos agrupamentos humanos' [was never able to maintain a psychological attitude towards the isolated man, but he knew surprisingly well how to penetrate human groups].[13] Nelson Werneck Sodré once again repeats that assumption, positively remarking on Azevedo's 'orquestração do meio coletivo' [orchestration of the collective environment].[14] Alfredo Bosi is perhaps the most explicit of all: 'Só em O Cortiço Aluísio atinou de fato com a fórmula que se ajustava ao seu talento: desistindo de montar um enredo em função de pessoas, ateve-se à seqüência de descrições muito precisas onde cenas coletivas e tipos psicologicamente primários fazem, no conjunto, do cortiço a personagem mais convincente do nosso romance naturalista' [Only in O Cortiço did Aluísio finally find the formula best suited to his talent: giving up the idea of creating a plot around *people*, he concentrated on very precise descriptions of collective scenes and psychologically primary types that transform, as a whole, the tenement into the most convincing character of our Naturalist novels].[15]

Here is another one of those fortunate phrases, used by Lúcia Miguel-Pereira and much repeated ever since: the tenement as 'the most convincing character' in the novel of Brazilian Naturalism. As all fortunate phrases, it allows us to understand, in one stroke, the weight of the collective scenes in the novel, as well as the great importance that space has in it. Moreover, it implies that space and people, in the case of this novel, are inextricably linked. Yet, as often happens with fortunate phrases, it also keeps us from going further into the analysis of the novel. Just like the much-repeated idea that collective movement is the best, if not the only good element of O Cortiço, the notion that the tenement itself is the novel's strongest character limits us to the surface of the phenomena described in it; in other words, it keeps us at the level of the 'exterior elements' mentioned by Sodré with respect to the Naturalists themselves. Because what is implicit — and in some cases explicit — in the assumptions that the tenement is the best character and collective movement the best overall aspect of the novel, is that Azevedo resorted to them because he could not create psychologically complex individual characters. As readers, we are then asked no more than to

---

[12] Miguel-Pereira, p. 149.
[13] Álvaro Lins, 'Dois Naturalistas: Aluísio Azevedo e Júlio Ribeiro', *Jornal de Crítica. 2a. Série* (Rio de Janeiro: José Olympio, 1943), pp. 134–65 (p. 149).
[14] Werneck Sodré, p. 189.
[15] Alfredo Bosi, *História Concisa da Literatura Brasileira* (São Paulo: Cultrix, 1994), p. 190.

observe the 'spectacle of the masses' and spy on the novel's 'best character', the tenement: the novel is colourful, brings us close to the people, but has no depth. This is perhaps the reason why O Cortiço, in spite of being considered one of the best novels in Brazilian literature, has received very few detailed analyses of its social processes, its structure, or indeed almost any other of its aspects. It has deserved, in other words, a treatment very similar to that accorded to Zola's novels until the 1950s — that is, a lack of engagement with the text itself on the part of the critics, who have tended to repeat the same set phrases already used to analyse Zola — even though, unlike Zola's texts, it was considered a good novel. An important exception is Antonio Candido's superb article 'De cortiço a cortiço', the first study to take seriously Azevedo's engagement with 'o mundo do trabalho, do lucro, da competição, da exploração econômica visível' [the world of labour, profit, competition, visible economic exploitation].[16] Even so, for Candido there is 'pouco sentimento de injustiça social e nenhum da exploração de classe, mas nacionalismo e xenofobia, ataque ao *abuso* do imigrante que vem "tirar o nosso sangue"' [little sense of social injustice in the novel and none of class exploitation, just nationalism and xenophobia, an attack on the immigrant's abuse, who has come here to 'drain our blood'].[17] By examining in detail how space is configured in the novel, I hope to show that O Cortiço actually reveals a deep sense of social injustice and class exploitation.

The problem is not only that the tenement is not, in any normal sense, a character, but that Azevedo's novel, besides its much-celebrated collective scenes (which proportionately form only a minor part of the text), is also composed of many individual characters, in fact some of the best-remembered characters in Brazilian literature. Such is the case of Rita Bahiana who conquered a definitive space in Brazilian minds as the sexy mulatta who drives men to commit the craziest acts, just to watch her move her hips while dancing the *chorado*. Rita even has literary daughters: Jorge Amado's Gabriela, for instance, is a direct continuation of Azevedo's mulatta: both share the same mixed-blood beauty, the lustrous hair perfumed with natural spices, the same open generosity and love of freedom. João Romão, the penny-pinching Portuguese immigrant is also a memorable character from O Cortiço, and so are the young prostitute Pombinha and the slave Bertoleza — all of them well remembered precisely because, I should add, they are types or caricatures. The fact that these and other characters in O Cortiço supposedly lack psychological depth does not make the relationship between them unimportant with respect to sexual and identity negotiations, as Mendes demonstrated,[18] or from the point of view of social and economic structures.

If we then go back to the idea of the tenement as a *character* and try to

---

[16] Antonio Candido, 'De cortiço a cortiço', in *O Discurso e a Cidade* (São Paulo: Duas Cidades, 1998), pp. 123–52 (p. 151).
[17] Candido, p. 131.
[18] Leonardo Mendes, *O Retrato do Imperador: Negociação, Sexualidade e Romance Naturalista no Brasil* (Porto Alegre: EDIPUCRS, 2000), p. 41.

unfold it, recovering its double reference to *space* and *people*, and if at the same time we expand the idea of 'people' to include not just crowds but the relationships between individuals, we can start to read the novel as a quite well-accomplished analysis of economic power as it is inscribed in the urban space of Rio de Janeiro. At the time, Brazil was slowly emerging from slavery with a series of laws that led to Abolition (1888) and the Republic (1889), the massive urbanization that drew in immigrants both within the country and from Europe, and the consequences all this had for the national imaginary of environment.

In contrast to Zola, and in spite of some critics' references to its 'detailed descriptions',[19] Azevedo's novel includes relatively few such, most of the novel consisting of dramatic action and dialogue. Above all, O *Cortiço* has no long descriptions in the style of Zola, much less of the type criticized by Lukács — the type that details one place or scene from more than one point of view.[20] Some of the most clearly descriptive passages in the novel are the formulaic passages, quoted above, that compare Brazilian nature (the jungle) to its Portuguese counterpart. The descriptions of city environment, in contrast, are brief and to the point, minimalist in the way they link the things or places described to a necessity created by the plot. One of the longest, for instance, depicts the quarry as João Romão is showing it to a possible new manager, Jerônimo. It is a panoramic scene that shows the rock face but above all the groups of men, and it is important because it allows Jerônimo to persuade João Romão to hire him on the basis that the job is presently being badly done (pp. 49–50 [pp. 34–35]). Again, when João Romão starts to build the tenement, all we know about the little houses is that they have two rooms and are badly built: we are told much more about the process of building, about how João Romão and Bertoleza steal materials and tools from the neighbourhood and hide them in the backyard. It is only when the tenement is completed that we are finally given a brief description of its floor plan, and even then only because the narrator needs to explain how it stood in relation to Miranda's house:

> E os quartos do cortiço pararam enfim de encontro ao muro do negociante, formado com a continuação da casa deste um grande quadrilongo, espécie de pátio de quartel, onde podia formar um batalhão.
> Noventa e cinco casinhas comportou a imensa estalagem. (p. 25)

> [The two-room houses finally stopped when they reached Miranda's wall and turned again to create a large quadrangle, one side of which was right up against his backyard. The space in the middle resembled the courtyard at a military barracks, large enough for an entire battalion to drill in.
> Ninety-five houses made up the huge slum.] (p. 11)

---

[19] See for instance Luiz Antonio Ferreira, *Roteiro de Leitura: 'O Cortiço' de Aluísio Azevedo* (São Paulo: Ática, 1997), p. 132, and Wilson Martins, *História da Inteligência Brasileira*, 7 vols (São Paulo: Cultrix; EDUSP: 1977), IV, 341.
[20] Georg Lukács, 'Narrate or Describe?', in *Writer and Critic and Other Essays*, ed. and trans. by Arthur D. Kahn (New York: Grosset and Dunlap, 1970), pp. 110–48 (p. 113).

Another example: when the active tenement is described for the first time — also one of the longest descriptions in the novel — it is through a panoramic scene that shows the movements of men and women going from the houses to the bathrooms and to the faucets to wash themselves, and from there to the shop to buy bread. Though highly visual in a choreographic sense, this scene includes few details about the place itself. The details of the scene prepare the reader for the arrival of each of the washerwomen. The novel does not give us a single description of the interior of the little houses in the tenement, except, at the end, of the unit rented by the homosexual washerman Albino, whose bed is always full of ants (p. 202 [p. 181]).

Space in *O Cortiço* is made up of people: their relationship with each other, the back-and-forth of their movements through the patio, the up-and-down views between Miranda's rich mansion and the tiny houses, the sounds of music, fights, and love-making as they are heard by anxious listeners. If we try to find the spatial model to represent this idea it will certainly not be the Euclidean notion of absolute space. The Aristotelian categories could be more useful (for we can basically talk about unity of space in *O Cortiço*), but they bring with them an unhelpful tendency to separate space from time and from other narrative elements, which is not appropriate, not even provisionally, to Azevedo's novel. Neither can space in it be depicted as a container inside which stories develop. Rather, the notion that can most usefully guide us through Azevedo's novel is Henri Lefebvre's 'social space', which as he explains in a self-conscious tautology, 'is a social product'.[21] As he defends the need for his space-centred approach, Lefebvre starts with Marx's replacement of 'this study of things taken "in themselves", in isolation from one another, with a critical analysis of productive activity itself (social labour; the relations and mode of production)'. He then goes on to claim that 'A comparable approach is called for today, an approach which would analyse not things in space but space itself, with a view to uncovering the social relationships embedded in it'.[22]

At the most basic level, *O Cortiço* can be described as a novel *about* the production of space, as it tells the story of how João Romão, a Portuguese immigrant of humble origins and little education, makes a fortune by building a tenement and renting each of its tiny units to families and individuals. Along with Bertoleza, the Black lover whom he pretended to have freed from slavery, he initially builds the tenement with his own hands, using materials stolen from the quarry behind the plot and from other construction sites. With time, the profits from the rent of the little houses allow him to buy the quarry, taking him another step towards controlling the means of production of space. Moreover, João Romão owns the shop where the tenants buy their food and other supplies, contracting debts that make them economically dependent on

---

[21] Henri Lefebvre, *The Production of Space*, trans. by Donald Nicholson-Smith (Oxford: Blackwell, 2000), p. 26.
[22] Ibid., p. 89.

him. Thus, João Romão is not simply the builder of the physical space tenement: he is the creator and controller of a social space. Needless to say, João Romão's tenement is part of a bigger process of production, the urbanization of the growing city of Rio de Janeiro. Botafogo, where the tenement is located, nowadays a central neighbourhood in Rio, was at the time part of the outskirts that were being incorporated into the city. This process followed a pattern typical of sudden urban growth: it was related to migration, both internal, of north-easterners who went to Rio in search of a better life, and external, of Portuguese and Italian immigrants.[23] It is also related to the nascent industrialization of the country, which is represented in the novel by the pasta and candle factories where some of the tenants work. The inhabitants of the tenement are, in the main, new to the city. They are also mostly poor workers, members of a new free workforce that was progressively replacing slave labour in the few years that preceded Abolition. The novel gives a clear view of the relationship between the tenement and the new economic conditions that are producing urban sprawl:

> Entretanto, a rua lá fora povoava-se de um modo admirável. Construía-se mal, porém muito; surgiam chalés e casinhas da noite para o dia; subiam os aluguéis; as propriedades dobravam de valor. Montara-se uma fábrica de massas italianas e outra de velas, e os trabalhadores passavam de manhã e às ave-marias, e a maior parte deles ia comer à casa de pasto que João Romão arranjara aos fundos da sua varanda. (p. 23)
>
> [Meanwhile, the street filled with people at an astonishing rate. The construction was shoddy, but there was a great deal of it. Shacks and small houses sprang up overnight. Rents rose, and properties doubled in value. An Italian pasta factory was built, and another that made candles. Workers trudged by each morning, at noon, and again in the evening, and most of them ate at the cheap eating-house he [João Romão] had set up under the veranda behind his store.] (pp. 9–10)

In the words of Lefebvre, 'If there is such a thing as the history of space, if space may indeed be said to be specified on the basis of historical periods, societies, modes of production and relations of production, then there is such a thing as a space characteristic of capitalism — that is characteristic of a society that is run

---

[23] According to Ribeiro, 'no período 1870/1890 ocorreu uma extraordinária expansão da população da cidade. Em 18 anos, com efeito, ela cresceu 90%' [in the period between 1870/1890 there was an extraordinary population growth in the city [of Rio de Janeiro]. In eighteen years, in fact, it grew by 90%]. However, 'tal crescimento demográfico não é acompanhado por uma correspondente expansão do parque domiciliar, aumentando, consequentemente, a densidade domiciliar no conjunto da cidade' [this growth was not followed by an expansion in the number of residences. Consequently the housing density grew significantly in the city as a whole]. Luiz Cesar de Queiroz Ribeiro, *Dos Cortiços aos Condomínios Fechados: As Formas de Produção da Moradia na Cidade do Rio de Janeiro* (Rio de Janeiro: Civilização Brasileira, 1997), pp. 169–73.

and dominated by the bourgeoisie'.[24] But can we call the filthy, penny-pinching João Romão a proper bourgeois? At first, this seems an unlikely prospect. In the earlier parts of the novel he sleeps with Bertoleza in a dirty room and works night and day. Despite all his wealth, he does not enjoy any of the comforts associated with bourgeois life: he dresses badly, eats little and cheap food, and does not drink good wine. His only drive is to make money: money that is used to make more and more money. In the words of the narrator: 'Desde que a febre de possuir se apoderou dele totalmente, todos os seus atos, todos, fosse o mais simples, visavam um interesse pecuniário. Só tinha uma preocupação: aumentar os bens' (p. 23) [Ever since this fever to possess had taken hold of him, all his actions, however simple, had pecuniary ends. He had one purpose only: to increase his wealth (p. 9)].[25] Described this way, João Romão's behaviour may seem to be that of a miser, but we should not be fooled by such appearances: in O Cortiço, the role of the miser is reserved, following the traditional anti-Jewish discourse of the time, to the old Jew, Libório. João Romão, by contrast, is a true capitalist, a man who knows the logic of money-making in a modern society. Marx himself points to the similarities between the capitalist and the miser: 'This urge towards absolute enrichment, this passionate hunt for value, is shared by the capitalist with the miser; but whereas the miser is only a capitalist gone mad, a capitalist is a miser who has come to his senses. The unceasing increment of value at which the miser aims in his endeavour to save his money from circulation, is attained by the shrewder capitalist by again and ever again handing over his money to circulation.'[26] Though not looking or living like a bourgeois, in the first part of the novel, João Romão embodies the logic of capitalism according to Marx, that is, his desire to produce capital is an end in itself, and has no limits.[27] For it is capital, not just money, that João Romão produces, in a process that begins with his selling food in a small grocery shop inherited from his former boss; it continues with the exploitation of the labour and savings of the slave Bertoleza (supposedly freed by him) in order to transform land into money-producing rental units — the tenement; and reaches a true capitalist stage, still quite early in the novel, with the incorporation of the space of the quarry for the production of building materials through the exploitation of a salaried workforce. According to the narrator, it is precisely when João Romão starts to employ workers in the quarry that he becomes truly rich: 'Pôs lá seis homens a quebrarem pedra e outros seis a fazerem lajedos e paralelepípedos, e então principiou a ganhar em grosso, tão em grosso que,

---

[24] Lefebvre, p. 126.

[25] In the English edition by David H. Rosenthal, the first sentence actually reads 'Ever since this fever to possess land had taken hold of him, all his actions, however simple, had pecuniary ends'. I have eliminated the word 'land' in order to make it closer to the Portuguese original.

[26] Karl Marx, *Capital Vol. 1*, trans. from the fourth German edition by Eden and Cedar Paul, 2 vols (London: Everyman's Library, 1967), I, 139.

[27] Ibid., I, 137.

dentro de ano e meio, arrematava já todo o espaço compreendido entre as suas casinhas e a pedreira, isto é, umas oitenta braças de fundo sobre vinte de frente em plano enxuto e magnífico para construir' (p. 17) [He hired six men to wield pickaxes and another six to fashion paving stones, and then he really began to make money — so much money that within a year and a half, he had bought up all the land between his row of houses and the quarry: that is, a plot about 500 by 120 feet, level, dry, and ideal for construction (pp. 4–5)]. Here is how Marx and Engels define 'capital' in 'Wage Labour and Capital': 'How, then, does any amount of commodities, of exchange values, become capital? By maintaining and multiplying itself as an independent social power, that is, as the power of a portion of society, by means of its exchange for direct living labour power. The existence of a class which possesses nothing but its capacity to labour is a necessary prerequisite of capital.'[28] By acquiring the means of social production (the quarry) and by exploiting labour, João Romão becomes a capitalist. And the prerequisite for his transformation are the workers, who also become the tenants of his tenement.

'Circulation' is an important concept in the novel, as the narrator again and again emphasizes how João Romão's capital is invested in order to create more capital. It is also linked to the general frantic movement that characterizes the novel, with people moving around the tenement and between the tenement and the shop, the eatery, the quarry. Merchandise is said to 'não lhe paravam nas prateleiras; o balcão estava cada vez mais lustroso, mais gasto. E o dinheiro a pingar, vintém por vintém, dentro da gaveta, e a escorrer da gaveta para a burra, aos cinqüenta e aos cem mil-réis, e da burra para o banco, aos contos e aos contos' (p. 23) [not to stay put on his shelves, and the counter where it was sold grew shinier and more worn. The coins rang as they tumbled into his till, whence they flooded into this strongbox in larger denominations and finally to the bank as *contos* (p. 10)]. But the money does not stay in the bank either, as João Romão hires new clerks, starts to buy products directly from Europe and, as he becomes even richer, expands his shop into a bazaar with more space and more workers, that make him even richer, and so on.

In the second half of the novel he 'comes to his senses', to use Marx's expression, by adopting a lifestyle more in line with his accumulated capital: he cleans up his appearance, and initiates a slow process of change that will culminate in his promise to marry the daughter of his rich neighbour, the recently ennobled baron Miranda. He now shaves and bathes everyday, wears clean and well-cut clothes, reads the newspapers, goes to concerts, and is seen in the central streets of Rio investing in the stock exchange. By the end of the novel he has become so prosperous that he provides goods for all the stores in Botafogo. More than that,

---

[28] Karl Marx and Friedrich Engels, 'Wage Labour and Capital' in *Selected Works in One Volume* (London: Lawrence and Wishart, 1968), pp. 64–93 (p. 81).

> A sua casa tinha agora um pessoal complicado de primeiros, segundos e terceiros caixeiros, além do guarda-livros, do comprador, do despachante e do caixa; do seu escritório saíam correspondências em várias línguas e, por dentro das grades de madeira polida, onde havia um bufete sempre servido com presunto, queijo, e cerveja, faziam-se largos contratos comerciais, transações em que se arriscavam fortunas; e propunham-se negociações de empresas e privilégios obtidos do governo; e realizavam-se vendas e compras de papéis; e concluíam-se empréstimos de juros fortes sobre hipotecas de grande valor. (p. 220)

> [his employees now included clerks of all ranks, as well as a bookkeeper, a buyer, a dispatcher and a receiver; his office carried on correspondence in several languages, and behind its grille of polished wood, by a sideboard always loaded with ham, cheese, and beer, detailed contracts were drawn up, fortunes were gambled, deals were made and privileges obtained from the government, certificates were bought and sold, and loans were granted at high interest rates secured by enormous collateral.] (p. 198)

The list of people that 'passed through his office' includes not only businessmen and brokers, but all kinds of charity officials, lawyers, and also 'foremen coming to collect the pay for João Romão's workers' (p. 220 [p. 198]).

At this point, his most troublesome physical connection with the old times is Bertoleza, who continues to sleep in the house. In order to get rid of her and marry Miranda's daughter, he considers setting up a vegetable shop for her in another part of the city, but she refuses the deal with a remarkable speech:

> — Ah! agora não me enxergo! agora eu não presto para nada! Porém, quando você precisou de mim não lhe ficava mal servir-se do meu corpo e agüentar a sua casa com o meu trabalho! Então a negra servia para um tudo; agora não presta para mais nada, e atira-se com ela no monturo do cisco! Não! assim também Deus não manda! Pois se aos cães velhos não se enxotam, por que me hão de pôr fora desta casa, em que meti muito suor do meu rosto?... Quer casar, espere então que eu feche primeiro os olhos; não seja ingrato! (p. 218)

> ['Ah! So now I'm good for nothing! But when you did need me, you didn't mind using my body in bed and my work to run your business! Then your nigger came in handy in all kinds of ways, but now when she's worn out you want to throw her out with the garbage! That's not right! People don't kick out old dogs, so who said you could kick me out of this house I helped build with the sweat of my brow! If you want to get married, wait till I'm dead; show a little respect!'] (p. 195)

João Romão dismisses the claim as absolutely insane and unreasonable. At the end, he takes advantage of the fact that he had never truly bought her freedom and calls the descendants of her former master to come and retrieve her. In an ending that Bosi called too theatrical, Aluísio has Bertoleza kill herself in order not to go back to being a slave, while João Romão, in another room, welcomes to his house a group of abolitionists who came to 'respectfully deliver a certificate declaring him an honored member and patron' [p. 208].

The message is all too clear: João Romão's new, gentrified tenement stands on the blood of slave labour. Modern capitalism and liberal ideas, in their Brazilian version, cannot erase its connections with slave money. Miguel-Pereira, who admired Bertoleza's dignity and her tragic suicide, lamented that 'o livro não termine aí, que o autor julgue necessário forçar a nota dramaticamente irônica, fazendo chegar uma comissão de abolicionistas para entregar a João Romão o diploma de sócio benemérito de sua sociedade' [the book didn't finish there, that the author should find it necessary to force the dramatically ironic tone by making an abolitionist commission arrive to give João Romão a certificate of contributing member of their society].[29] I disagree: though the scene does have a theatrical feel to it, it also has an important function. When the novel came out, two years after Abolition, it would have been easy to dismiss João Romão, after his turning Bertoleza over to her former master, as a backward supporter of slavery. In contrast, by depicting him as an abolitionist, Azevedo is able to criticize not simply an old order, which had already been replaced, but the new. João Romão is Brazilian modernity in its combination of fully capitalist exploitation of a salaried workforce (and, we should add, its participation in a global market), with its still recent economic ties with slavery and its refusal to recognize, after Abolition, that the former slaves were owed an equal part of its new, modern life.

Far from being simply a miser fatefully driven by an abnormal desire to acquire wealth — as he is initially described and as indeed many critics, repeating accusations of fatalism made against Zola, were quick to accept — João Romão is the embodiment of an economic process — capitalism, with its own dynamic. 'The circulation of money as capital' is, as Marx puts it, 'an end in itself, for the expansion of value can only occur within this perpetually renewed movement. Consequently, the circulation of capital has no limits.'[30]

Whether or not Azevedo knew Marx's texts is a question that can probably never be answered. The 'Communist Manifesto' was translated into French (a language all Brazilian writers had to read) in 1848, and *Capital* in 1872.[31] Zola's *Germinal* quotes Marx and makes use of his economic theories, even though it does not subscribe to the latter's quasi-religious belief in the Revolution. In any case, in the second half of the nineteenth century socialist ideas were in the air and were almost certainly known, though not in depth, by many people who had not read any of the original texts. More importantly, Marx's were not the only socialist theories around, as the works of Saint-Simon and Proudhon enjoyed popularity in Latin America. The latter is particularly relevant here for the extremely famous beginning of his book *What is Property?*, much quoted at the time:

[29] Miguel-Pereira, p. 151.
[30] Marx, *Capital*, I, 137.
[31] For a history of the reception of socialist texts in Brazil see José Nilo Tavares, *Marx, o Socialismo e o Brasil* (Rio de Janeiro: Civilização Brasileira, 1983).

> If I had to answer the following question, 'What is slavery?' and if I should respond in one word, 'It is murder', my meaning would be understood at once. I should not need a long explanation to show that the power to deprive a man of his thought, his will, and his personality is the power of life and death. So why to this other question, 'What is property?' should I not answer in the same way, 'It is theft', without fearing to be misunderstood, since the second proposition is only a transformation of the first?[32]

Slavery and theft are also represented as twin principles in O Cortiço, since the economic progress of João Romão depended, initially, on the money and work of Bertoleza, and on the theft of tools, building materials, and even bits of land. Theft continued to be a common practice for João Romão throughout his career — as we can see after the fire that destroys the tenement, when he steals money from the old Libório, and on many other occasions.

Through João Romão, Aluísio Azevedo discusses the hegemony of the bourgeoisie over the free and enslaved working classes of Rio de Janeiro in the final decades of the nineteenth century — a hegemony that is, as we should expect, inscribed in space. Following Lefebvre, let us ask: what kind of space was produced by a bourgeoisie that at that stage still relied on slavery, and that would continue to rely on its legacy of extremely cheap labour and servitude even after abolition? One possible answer might be: the tenement, though not the tenement in isolation.

Spatial Practices

First, in sheer physical terms the tenement is not isolated because of the proximity of its tiny houses to Miranda's imposing mansion. Such overlapping of wealth and poverty follows a visual logic of verticality: the mansion looks at the tenement from above, while the latter observes the inhabitants of the house from below. As Lefebvre puts it, 'The arrogant verticality of skyscrapers, and especially of public and state buildings, introduces a phallic or more precisely, a phallocentric element into the visual realm; the purpose of this display, of this need to impress, is to convey an impression of authority to each spectator. Verticality and great height have ever been the spatial expression of potentially violent power'.[33] Of course we cannot talk about 'skyscrapers' or 'public and state buildings' in the case of O Cortiço, but the need to 'convey an impression of authority in each spectator' is still there. So much so that João Romão's great ambition when he changes his life style is to build 'um sobrado mais alto que o do Miranda, e, com toda a certeza, mais vistoso' (p. 191) [a house taller than Miranda's and far more imposing (p. 171)]. And if it is true that we cannot deny the theatrical effects and narrative advantages of having the mansion and the tenement sharing, so to speak, the same space, it is also true that such superimposition corresponds to the actual social contrast of Rio, visible still

---

[32] Pierre-Joseph Proudhon, *What is Property?*, ed. and trans. by Donald. R. Kelley and Bonnie G. Smith. (Cambridge: Cambridge University Press, 1993), p. 13.

[33] Lefebvre, p. 98.

today in the *favelas* that hang from the hillsides, face to face with the inhabitants of luxurious condominiums. Nowadays, however, we can speak of an inverted visual logic of verticality, or maybe even of a battle for verticality in a city where tall apartment buildings compete with the mountain slums.

In *O Cortiço*, the relationship between the inhabitants of the mansion and those of the tenement takes several forms, all of them denouncing, at various levels, class difference. Thus, the poor washerwomen become, for example, the object of voyeuristic desire by male members of the mansion, particularly by Henrique, the young lodger of Miranda's household. He repeatedly watches Pombinha as she goes about in her daily tasks, and ends up having sex with one of the washerwomen, Leocádia, in an encounter arranged through gestures between the windows of the mansion and the patio of the tenement. The inhabitants of the tenement, too, like to observe what happens in the mansion. But instead of voyeuristic desires, they express a negative moral judgement about the rich family's behaviour, especially the adulterous encounters of Miranda's wife, Dona Estela. Here, Azevedo makes a clear distinction between the morality of the lower classes and that of the bourgeoisie. The latter's marriages are made exclusively on financial grounds. Miranda married Estela for her family's money, when he was still a poor immigrant recently arrived from Portugal;[34] João Romão got together with Bertoleza also for financial interest, and later arranged to marry Zulmira for the same reason. The result of such marriages can be disastrous, or at least it is in the case of Miranda and Estela, who hate each other. The poor, on the other hand — in spite of the narrator's occasional claims about promiscuity in the tenement, which is also seen as a breeding ground for prostitutes — are still capable of marrying for love, and seem much freer in their sexual and amorous choices. When a group in the tenement is gossiping about Miranda's desire to marry his daughter Zulmira to a rich man, the judgement is clear:

> — Por isso é que se vê tanta porcaria por esse mundo de Cristo! disse a Augusta. Filha minha só se casará com quem ela bem quiser; que isto de casamentos empurrados à força acabam sempre desgraçando tanto a mulher como o homem! Meu marido é pobre e é de cor, mas eu sou feliz, porque casei por meu gosto!
> — Ora, mais vale um gosto que quatro vinténs! (p. 75)

---

[34] The relationship between Miranda and Estela resembles in many aspects the marriage between Monsieur and Madame Hennebeau in *Germinal*. Both husbands got to where they are now because of the adulterous relationships of their wives in the city. Both wives continue to have amorous encounters in the new house, and both end up having as lovers very young lodgers, a nephew in the case of Madame Hennebeau, and a customer's son in the case of Miranda. In addition, both husbands retain some kind of fascination towards their wives: in the case of Monsieur Hennebeau, it is expressed in a continuing sexual desire that is never materialized because he is afraid of being despised by her; in the case of Miranda, he cannot resist his needs and goes to his wife's room once a month, so that 'from then on their sexual relations were better than ever, though their dislike of each other had in no way diminished' (p. 7).

> ['That's why there are so many sluts in the world!' Augusta added. 'My daughter's going to marry someone she loves; forced marriages always turn out badly for the woman and the man. My husband's poor and colored, but I'm happy because he's the one I wanted to marry.'
> 'Damned right! Money isn't everything!'] (p. 58)

The actual exchanges between the inhabitants of the mansion and those from the tenement also put in evidence the feelings each class has towards the other. On a Sunday, for instance, the parties at the tenement bother the inhabitants of the mansion, and Miranda comes to the window to protest:

> — Vão gritar pra o inferno, com um milhão de raios! berrou ele, ameaçando para baixo. Isto também já é demais! Se não se calam, vou daqui direito chamar a polícia! Súcia de brutos!
> Com os berros do Miranda muita gente chegou à porta da casa, e o coro de gargalhadas, que ninguém podia conter naquele momento de alegria, ainda mais o pôs fora de si.
> — Ah, canalhas! O que eu devia fazer é atirar-lhes daqui, como a cães danados! (p. 70)

> ['God damn you all, why don't you do your yelling in hell?' he roared, threatening those below him. 'This is going too far! If you don't shut up, I'll call the police, you lousy brutes!'
> Miranda's shouts brought people to their doors, and their uncontrollable laughter made him still more furious.
> 'Scum! I should shoot you all like rabid dogs!'] (p. 54)

The adjectives he uses (*súcia de brutos, canalhas, cães danados*) confirm his sense of superiority towards his neighbours, while the inhabitants of the tenement respond with irreverence, or, in the case of the troublemaker Firmo, Rita's boyfriend, with violent threats: '— Facilita muito, meu boi manso, que te escorvo os galhos na primeira ocasião' (p. 71) ['You chicken-hearted son of a bitch, I'll cut you down to size the first chance I get!' (p. 54)] — a remark that provokes panic in Miranda's family, who take him away from the window. Later, when Miranda's household is celebrating his becoming a baron, it is the noise of champagne bottles and shouts from the mansion that provoke the resentful protest from the inhabitants of the tenement.

In addition to Miranda's mansion, several networks relate the tenement to the city around it, following the 'law' mentioned by Lefebvre, according to which 'Social spaces interpenetrate one another and/or superimpose themselves upon one another'.[35] As a social space, the tenement is the result of various spatial practices. First among them is the planning of João Romão, who conceives and builds it, on the one hand, piling the highest possible number of rent-paying inhabitants into the smallest possible space. According to Ribeiro, the building of *cortiços* in Rio de Janeiro between 1870s and 1890s was 'regulada tão-somente pela busca da apropriação de uma renda fundiária, na forma de aluguel de

---

[35] Lefebvre, p. 86.

cômodos ou de pequenos cortiços, casas de cômodos e estalagens. Para tanto, o "corticeiro" procura investir o mínimo possível e aproveitar ao máximo o terreno' [regulated only by the desire to acquire property income in the form of room rental or the rental of small tenement houses. For this purpose, the landlord invested as little as possible and occupied as much of the land as he could].[36] Indeed, the urban sprawl caused by the nascent industrialization of Rio guarantees João Romão a permanent revenue from the little houses: 'À proporção que alguns locatários abandonavam a estalagem, muitos pretendentes surgiram disputando os cômodos desalugados [...] Os números dos hóspedes crescia, os casulos subdividiam-se em cubículos do tamanho de sepulturas (p. 145) [As soon as any tenant left São Romão, a crowd of candidates appeared, all squabbling over the vacant house. [...] The number of inhabitants increased; each two-room house was subdivided into cubicles the size of coffins (p. 125)].

On the other hand, this modern urban building logic is combined with the remnants of provincial town planning, so that the initial ninety-five houses are built around a courtyard 'onde podia formar um batalhão' (p. 25) [large enough for an entire battalion to drill in (p. 11)]. This planning serves to accommodate an older form of economy which has its origins in slavery and that coexisted with nascent capitalism in late nineteenth-century Brazil: the rental of wash tubs to professional *lavadeiras* (washerwomen). This includes, of course, most female tenants but also many washerwomen from outside the tenement. Such a design generates in turn its own spatial practices: as a public space, the courtyard serves as the social centre of the tenement. Our first encounter with the inhabitants of the tenement, for instance, happens through the women, who appear, one by one, in the washing scene. The washing tubs also relate the women of the tenement with other parts of the city, for they all do the laundry of wealthier families. Such networks between laundry women and the families they work for are made visible at a few moments in the novel, when owners or servants from the wealthier houses come looking for their clothes. The washing tubs also establish a relationship between the public space of the patio and the private space of the house. Ironically, washing laundry is a definition of the private, as in the expression 'don't wash dirty linen in public', a recommendation that cannot be taken literally in a society that, due to a long history of slavery, came to rely on the service of poorly paid labour to accomplish the daily tasks of the house. Thus the clothes of the best families in Rio were hung out to dry in the public spaces of the tenement, erasing not only the limits between the private and the public, but more specifically, between the private of the richer and the public of the working class. But the women also 'wash their own linen' in the public space of the patio, as their conversations around the washing-tubs often refer to personal and sexual topics. Thus, the whole tenement knows, for instance, that the eighteen-

---

[36] Queiroz Ribeiro, p. 205.

year-old Pombinha, the flower of the tenement, has not yet become sexually mature. When she finally does, her mother, the washerwoman Dona Isabel, all but exhibits as a banner the blood of her menstruation, once again relating the theme of laundry-washing and personal life.

At night, the patio of the tenement becomes less a communal setting than an unwittingly shared space. Once again, private and public are difficult to distinguish, as various social gatherings are heard or observed by those who have and have not been invited. This is a typically urban scenario of welcome and unwelcome sounds and smells that generate multiple desires and anxieties. It is here that the conflicts between the different ethnic groups that live in the tenement are acted out. The Brazilians are represented mainly by the mulatta Rita Bahiana, her lover Firmo and their various friends who play and dance the *chorado*. Against them we have Portuguese immigrants like Jerônimo and his wife Piedade, who long for their cool, distant villages, while playing nostalgic fados. The Italians constitute the third ethnic group, but they always appear together and are invariably described by the noise they make and the amount of litter they produce.

As with most urban spaces, this tenement brings together individuals of different origins, and the conflicts between them allow Azevedo to adapt the determinist logic that Naturalism is credited with to the Brazilian environment. Hence, hard-working and ethical Portuguese such as Jerônimo become lazy, drunk, and sexually obsessed when exposed to the warmth of the tropical sun. Jerônimo falls in love with Rita because 'Naquela mulata estava o grande mistério, a síntese das impressões que ele recebeu chegando aqui: ela era a luz ardente do meio-dia; ela era o calor vermelho das sestas da fazenda; era o aroma quente dos trevos e das baunilhas, que o atordoara nas matas brasileiras; era a palmeira virginal e esquiva que se não torce a nenhuma outra planta; era o veneno e era o açúcar gostoso' (p. 78) [That mulatta embodied the mystery, the synthesis of everything he had experienced since his arrival in Brazil. She was the blazing light of midday; the fierce heat of the farm where he had toiled; the pungent scent of clover and vanilla that had made his head spin in the jungle; the palm tree, proud and virginal, unbending before its fellow plants. She was poison and sugar (p. 61)]. But as Mendes observed, in the case of O *Cortiço* such claims are surprisingly ambiguous. If it is true that Jerônimo is described at first as being strong, honest, and responsible, and his wife as being naturally beautiful, virtuous, and hard-working, it is also true that their music is presented as boring, their food bland and uninteresting, and their bodies as lacking personal hygiene. The mulatta Rita Bahiana, on the other hand, is depicted as being too fond of a good time: she often abandons work in order to accompany her boyfriend Firmo in orgies that last weeks. But she is also open, generous, and happy, her hair smells of vanilla and nobody in the tenement, man, woman, or child, can resist her charms. Firmo, it is true, is closer to being a villain: he is a violent *capoeira* fighter who is always looking for trouble. But he is also a brilliant musician, and his tendency to violence ends up being no worse than that of Jerônimo, who kills him in a rather treacherous fight because of Rita.

It is this fight that causes the fire which ultimately destroys most of the tenement, the result of arson initiated by the mysterious Bruxa. The only indigenous character in the whole novel, this 'witch' is occasionally described as mad by the narrator, a sinister woman, but one who is nevertheless a wise herbalist and who can cure diseases. She twice attempts to burn the tenement down, and when she succeeds, in her second attempt, 'ela ria-se, ébria de satisfação, sem sentir as queimaduras e as feridas, vitoriosa no meio daquela orgia de fogo, com que ultimamente vivia a sonhar em segredo a sua alma extravagante de maluca' (p. 184) [She roared with laughter, indifferent to her burns, reveling in that orgy of flames, which she had dreamed of so long in secret (p. 163)]. This Indian woman who burns down João Romão's property cannot but remind us of the 'muralha de fogo com que o espírito eternamente revoltado do último tambor entricheirou a pátria contra os conquistadores aventureiros' [wall of fire behind which the last Tamoio Indian's rebellious spirit defends its fatherland against conquering adventurers from overseas], quoted near the beginning of this essay. It recalls, too, the celebrated climax of the Brazilian Indian's speech in Montaigne's essay 'Of Cannibals': '... that they had observed that there were among us men full and crammed with all sorts of things, while their halves were begging at their doors, emaciated with hunger and poverty, and they thought it strange that these necessitous halves were able to suffer such an injustice, and that they did not take the others by the throat or set fire to their houses'.[37] This symbolic role of the Indian woman supports an allegorical reading of the novel according to which João Romão embodies not only Brazilian modernity, as I already indicated, but the whole historical process that created such modernity, beginning with Portuguese theft and colonization of Indian land, exploitation of Black slaves, and finally, integration into a capitalist order based on free labour.[38]

Like a true capitalist João Romão does not lose any money with the fire: he had insured the tenement above its actual value, and managed to steal the life-savings of the old Libório, who died in the disaster. With the profits, he starts the process of gentrifying the tenement; instead of one, he now builds two stories of houses, with verandas:

> À esquerda, até onde acabava o prédio do Miranda, estendia-se um novo correr de casinhas de porta e janela, e daí por diante, acompanhando todo o lado do fundo e dobrando depois para a direita até esbarrar no sobrado de João Romão, erguia-se um segundo andar, fechado em cima do primeiro por uma estreita e extensa varanda de grades de madeira, para a qual se

---

[37] Michel de Montaigne, *The Essays of Michel de Montaigne*, trans. and ed. by Jacob Zeilin (New York: Alfred A. Knopf, 1936), p. 190.
[38] For the importance of allegory in Azevedo's novel, see Candido, 'De cortiço a cortiço'.

subia por duas escadas, uma em cada extremidade. De cento e tantos, a numeração dos cômodos elevou-se a mais de quatrocentos. (p. 202)

[On the left, by Miranda's house, there was a new row of doors and windows, and facing them, all along the back and then turning into another row that extended as far as João Romão's house, there was a second floor with a long wooden veranda and two sets of stairs: one at either end. Instead of a hundred or so, there were now more than four hundred dwellings.] (p. 181)

Middle-class service workers now move into the tenement, and many of the old-timers are forced to go live in 'Catheads', the neighbouring tenement that has gone the other way, becoming slummier. Here Azevedo describes another familiar urban process: the gentrification that displaces the poorer populations to worse parts of the city. Instead of a patio, the new tenement has an avenue between the rows of houses. Its purpose is not gathering, but circulation, that is, bring people in and out of the new tenement. With these changes, professionals start to open workshops in the tenement, and their clients, one imagines, are able to walk in and out safely. Due to the larger number of houses and the new spatial configuration, the inhabitants of the tenement are now less prone to mix private and public life: their parties happen inside their houses, and many of them do not mingle at all.

Social Control and Other Implications

As a social product, the tenement is also a space of control. In both its initial and gentrified shapes, the long row of houses allows João Romão (whose own house stands at the entrance of the tenement) to keep a close eye on the lives of the inhabitants, repressing them any time he sees fit. In his role as the owner of the tenement, he has the right to evict anybody that violates his authority in the use of space, and that right is never questioned by the inhabitants of the tenement. In other words, the spatial and social organization of the tenement is highly determined by the logic of rent monopoly, a logic that assures in daily practices the hegemony of one class over others. But cityscapes are spaces of contradiction, and while urban landscape can allow more control over individuals, it also creates its own pockets of resistance. If it is true that the inhabitants of the tenement cannot counter João Romão's rights as owner, it is also true that they are successful in counteracting the repressive state apparatus when, united by a common fear of the police, they actively repel, on more than one occasion, the attempts by policemen to enter the tenement. When the police finally come in, they do so with a vengeance, exhibiting a brutality that is unfortunately all too familiar to present-day Latin American cities.

In his descriptions of the tenement and its inhabitants, Azevedo at times resorts to some of the familiar tropes of Naturalism. Thus, the tenement is compared to a heap of dung, generating worms (the inhabitants), and few of the characters escape comparison with animals at one or other moment in the novel. As an environment, the tenement is also said to have an unavoidable influence over the people who live in it, such as Pombinha, as we have seen. Yet, for most of the novel Azevedo seems to go against these deterministic principles. As Mendes puts it: 'O Cortiço como um criadouro de prostitutas pode funcionar bem como preceito Naturalista, mas contradiz o que dizem quase todos os personagens do romance. As duas prostitutas do romance o são por escolha própria, e parecem felizes com sua escolha... Talvez as criaturas de O Cortiço não sejam uma boa ilustração para as teses Naturalistas do narrador' [O Cortiço as a hotbed for prostitutes works well as a Naturalist precept, but it goes against what almost every character in the novel says. The two prostitutes in the novel have become so by choice, and they seem happy with their choices [...] Maybe the creatures in O Cortiço are not good illustrations for the narrator's Naturalist theses].[39] Indeed, most of the characters in the novel are not simply influenced by the environment they live in, they also have an active role in producing it.

If in order to read Aluísio Azevedo we need to make reference to Zola it is not because of the 'fatalism' or 'determinism' of both authors, nor simply to compare the 'collective scenes' in their novels. The main lesson Azevedo seems to have learned from his French Master (apart, of course, from specific situations and certain similar characters) was the critique of the dominant economic and social order, which is done, in both authors, through a rupture with what Schor called the 'hegemony of the French psychological novel'.[40] In Zola, an extremely acute visual sense and very detailed descriptions create a world where people seem dwarfed by the things around them. And although those things are moveable as commodities to be consumed, they create a sense of space that is oppressive and unchangeable, reflecting a well-established social and economic order where upward movement by the poor, although promised, is actually very rare. In Azevedo, short, almost schematic descriptions of objects and scenery serve as a minimal structure for a space that is made up of people and that is constantly being produced and changed by people. Their frantic movement mimics the infinite need for circulation of capitalism itself. This changeability of space reflects a social order in formation, where everything seems to be up for grabs, where ethnic and class identities are still being negotiated. The reason why the lack of descriptions in O Cortiço may have appealed to so many readers could have to do with the fact that in Brazil, unlike Zola's France, the upper classes did not need detailed descriptions to visualize the space of the poor: like the bourgeois women in the novel, all they had to do was to open their windows. The readers' interest in spaces of poverty like the tenement stemmed then not from a need to *see* those places, but from a desire to understand the choreography of identity and class negotiation in a society that

---

[39] Mendes, O Retrato do Imperador, p. 45.
[40] Schor, p. xiii.

was changing very fast. The permeability between the spaces of the rich and of the poor does not point, however, to a fairer relationship between the classes. On the contrary: it indicates that along with modern capitalist exploitation of free labour, there still remained in Brazilian society a slavery-derived tradition of servitude. Moreover, capitalist mobility itself is based, according to the novel, on brutal exploitation and theft. The fact that both writers chose to depict capitalism as a system that perpetuates class differences is not due to their fatalistic theories of human nature and society, but to a visionary understanding of capitalism's necessity and extraordinary ability to perpetuate itself.

UNIVERSITY OF MANCHESTER

The Brazil of Sílvio Romero and Machado de Assis: History of a 'Polemic', or the Writer as Critic of the Critic

ALBERTO SCHNEIDER

Introduction

The objective of this article is to explore the aesthetic and political tension between Sílvio Romero (1851–1914) — an important intellectual and literary critic from the end of the nineteenth century — and the writer Machado de Assis (1839–1908), his contemporary, who at this time enjoyed a notable prestige in Brazilian literary circles. Furthermore, the article suggests an inversion of roles, in presenting the work of Machado de Assis as an implicit critique of the interpretative principles adopted by Sílvio Romero, a historian and literary critic who shared with Machado de Assis not only his times, but his institutions and his readers. The terrain of the polemic — which never actually took place[1] — was the way in which each located himself within the intellectual debate that permeated the Brazil of the time, the country which each lived in and examined in their work.

Seen from the present day, there is a huge disparity between the literary prestige of Machado de Assis and the almost total disappearance of Sílvio Romero. In 1897, however, the year in which Romero published his book dedicated to Machado's work, the critic enjoyed a considerable intellectual reputation, wrote regularly for the best Rio de Janeiro newspapers, published books, and lectured in the prestigious *Colégio Pedro II*.

Observing how each positioned himself in the public debate on Brazilian nationality helps us to understand why Romero has faded from view, while Machado has endured. The latter's work can be read as a silent critique of conceptions adopted by the critic. As we shall try to demonstrate, Romero constructed an interpretation based on nationalism and scientism, two approaches dear to the second half of the nineteenth century, while Machado de Assis rejected that agenda.

Machado de Assis and Sílvio Romero lived and wrote in the same city, namely Rio de Janeiro, and they were witnesses to the end of the Empire

[1] In 1897, Sílvio Romero devoted a critical and hostile book to the work of Machado de Assis, who answered him with complete silence — in a time marked by great debates and intellectual confrontations. On this, see Roberto Ventura, *O estilo tropical: história intelectual e polêmica literária no Brasil, 1870–1914* (São Paulo: Companhia das Letras, 1991).

and of slavery, and to all the other transformations that the Brazil of that time underwent. They both published books and were read by the intelligentsia of the period, though no one in literary circles of the turn of the century enjoyed more prestige than Machado de Assis, founder and first president of the *Academia Brasileira de Letras*. Sílvio Romero was one of the intellectuals who, in 1897, founded that institution — even though he refused to take part in the day-to-day affairs of the Academy, because he regarded it as 'amorphous' and the den of the 'panelinha fluminense' [Rio coterie] clustered around the *Editora Garnier*. To Romero, the intellectual and literary atmosphere reflected the oligarchic spirit of the Brazilian political elite, within which Machado de Assis exercised a central role. The personal differences between them, both intellectual and political, were considerable.

It is important to recognize that history has weighed in favour of Machado de Assis. Contemporary literary sensibility is infinitely closer to Machado's legacy, while time has been less kind towards Sílvio Romero, given that his convictions, steeped in an ethnological and sociological determinism — in which concepts such as 'race' and 'miscegenation' operated as interpretative keys — have lost their validity. Sílvio Romero was a typical nineteenth-century intellectual, given to reading Brazil, and thus Brazilian literature, in a specific, individual way, but with the hegemonic intellectual tools of his day. His mental world was informed by a fixedly nationalist agenda, on the one hand, and a profound faith in progress and science on the other. Because he believed in unequal 'races', in which the whites occupied the top of the chain, he felt obliged to condemn miscegenation in the name of science, even though he showed some sympathy towards it. His faith in evolution and progress brought him to believe that 'a forma branca prevalece e prevalecerá' [the white race prevails and will prevail]:

> O mestiço é o produto fisiológico, étnico e histórico do Brasil; é a forma nova de nossa diferenciação nacional. Nossa psicologia popular é um produto desse estado inicial. *Não quero dizer que constituiremos uma nação de mulatos* [grifo nosso]; pois a forma branca prevalece e prevalecerá; quero dizer apenas que o europeu aliou-se aqui a outras raças, e desta união saiu o genuíno brasileiro, aquele que não se confunde mais com o português e sobre o qual repousa nosso futuro.[2]

> [The *mestiço* is the physiological, ethnic and historical product of Brazil; he is the new shape of our national differentiation. Our popular psychology is a product of that initial state. *I do not mean that we shall constitute a nation of mulattos* [my emphasis]; since the white race prevails and will prevail; I mean only that the European allied himself here with other races, and from this union emerged the genuine Brazilian, the one that is no longer confused with the Portuguese and upon which our future rests.]

---

[2] Sílvio Romero, *História da literatura brasileira*, 5 vols (Rio de Janeiro: José Olympio, 1953), III, 132.

Above all in his novels *Memórias póstumas de Brás Cubas* (1880), *Quincas Borba* (1891) and *Dom Casmurro* (1899), Machado de Assis rejected the ethnic determinism which had so troubled Brazilian and Latin American intellectuals of the nineteenth century. The Mexican writer Carlos Fuentes puts forward a shrewd interpretation: the strength of Machado de Assis may have lain in his capacity to free himself from the hegemonic perceptions of his time, finding in certain aspects of the Western literary tradition — and specifically the literary tradition descending from Miguel de Cervantes — the elements necessary to work through a creative rejection, or even a critique:

> el milagro se sostiene sobre una paradoja: Machado asume, en Brasil, la lección de Cervantes, la tradición de La Mancha que olvidaran, por más homenajes que cívica y escolarmente se rindiesen al Quijote, los novelistas hispanoamericanos de México.[3]

> [the miracle is based on a paradox: Machado adopts, in Brazil, the lesson of Cervantes, the tradition of La Mancha, which the Latin American novelists of Mexico, however much civic and scholarly homage they had paid to Quixote, had forgotten.]

This article aims to explore the conflict between Sílvio Romero and Machado de Assis from this angle. However, in order to understand the background to the question it is necessary to examine the historical and cultural terrain within which each was writing, the Brazil of the last quarter of the nineteenth century.

★ ★ ★ ★ ★

Between 1870 and the first years of the twentieth century, the country passed through a period of intense political, economic and social transformations. Even Independence, in 1822, had not brought such significant changes, since independent Brazil maintained an economic and social order based on the *latifundium* and slavery, as well as constructing a monarchical political model, based on the same House of Bragança.

However, from 1870 onwards changes become much more intense. The monarchy and slavery were openly contested, particularly by journalists, intellectuals, writers, doctors and lawyers, many of them the sons of rich plantation owners, educated in Europe, and more sensitive to the demands of the incipient urban middle class, which, in a cautious way, was starting to emerge from a still markedly rural society.

In the second half of the nineteenth century, the sugar produced on the Atlantic coast, especially the north-east of Brazil, was losing importance in comparison to the coffee cultivated in the provinces of Rio de Janeiro and São Paulo, bringing a concentration of political and economic power to this

---

[3] Carlos Fuentes, *Machado de la Mancha* (Mexico: Fondo de Cultura Económica, 2001), pp. 9–10.

region.[4] Rio de Janeiro, as well being the administrative capital and the biggest city in the country, had consolidated itself as the main cultural, political and economic centre in Brazil, drawing in educated people from the provinces and contributing to the creation of a fertile terrain for new political ideas.[5]

The abolition of slavery, in 1888, and the proclamation of the Republic, in 1889, brought many changes to the economic and social life of the country. Brazil went through a process of material and ideological modernization, although the Brazilian elite maintained intact its control of power. Increasingly, both the upper classes and the emerging middle classes looked for inspiration to the values and ways of life of contemporary Europe. It was not by chance that policies aimed at attracting European immigrants were implemented during this period. Between 1890 and 1900 alone — the decade following Abolition, at which point Brazil had had a little over 14 million inhabitants — some 1.4 million immigrants entered the country, double the number of arrivals over the previous eighty years (i.e. 1808–88).

If on the one hand these transformations raised expectations, the country was on the other hand experiencing a period of self-doubt and pessimism. The intellectuals of this period, mostly abolitionists and Republicans,[6] were strongly influenced by ideas very critical of Brazil's past, from the Romantic phase in literature to its colonial experience, experiencing profound doubts (and profound certainties) as to the ethnic characteristics of the population that made up the country.

This post-Romantic generation had a notably universalist outline, in the sense of adopting rationalist values, expressed in a realist or naturalist style. Intellectuals, including critics such as Sílvio Romero and José Veríssimo and writers such as Aluísio Azevedo and Euclides da Cunha, were interested in effecting a historical updating of Brazilian society, along markedly Westernizing lines; this meant a major turn towards the outward signs of modernity, characteristic of the second industrial revolution, with an emphasis on science, taken to be the main explicative nexus of 'reality'.[7]

The modernist generation of 1870, as Antônio Cândido called it,[8] engaged with and was affected by European intellectual life in the second half of the

[4] *A invenção do Brasil moderno*, ed. by Micael M. Herschman and Carlos Alberto Messeder Pereira (Rio de Janeiro: Rocco, 1994), pp. 9–42.

[5] Jeffrey D. Needell, *Belle époque tropical: sociedade e cultura de elite no Rio de Janeiro na virada do século* (São Paulo: Companhia das Letras, 1993).

[6] Amongst the main intellectuals of this period, there was practically a consensus on Abolition of slavery, but not on a Republic. The roll of well-known monarchists was long, starting with Machado de Assis himself, as well as Joaquim Nabuco, Oliveira Lima and Eduardo Prado, amongst others. They included intellectuals who were not necessarily conservative, as in the case of Joaquim Nabuco, who was a liberal, and leading abolitionists.

[7] See Nicolau Sevcenko, *Literatura como missão: tensões sociais e criação cultural na Primeira República* (São Paulo: Brasiliense, 1985).

[8] See Antônio Cândido, *O método crítico de Sílvio Romero* (São Paulo: Ed. da USP, 1963).

nineteenth century, then distinguished by a markedly anti-spiritualist and anti-metaphysical turn. At this time the influences of the positivism of Comte (1798–1857), the evolutionism of Spencer (1820–1903) and the monism of Haekel (1834–1919) set in motion a determinist tendency, characterized by the adoption of the founding principles of the natural sciences, of empirical knowledge and an experimental approach.[9] Young Brazilian intellectuals of the period read avidly from these authors, whose ideas arrived in Brazil just as slavery was exhausting itself, and which, paradoxically, served to give a scientific status to racism and to dull the aspiration to make citizens of former slaves.[10]

One of the topics tackled obsessively by Brazilian intellectuals was the question of 'race'. It was only in the nineteenth century, under the aegis of science, that this idea had been given biological and morphological criteria. It was no longer phenomena of a religious, linguistic, juridical or cultural order that defined 'race', but a belief that all these elements had a physical explanation.[11]

The seduction of the greater part of the Brazilian intelligentsia by a scientistic and frequently racist universalism led them to have doubts about the future of a country like Brazil, where a considerable portion of the population was black, indigenous or mixed-race. Miscegenation, a factor since the beginning of Portuguese colonization, was fiercely criticized by certain elements of European intellectual thought.[12] The acceptance of this 'science', based on the supposed superiority of the 'white race', suggested a problem that often damaged the confidence of Brazilian intellectuals in the future of their country.

All over the Western world, the end of the nineteenth century was a time of intense nationalist sensibility, in which intellectual debates over the supposedly intrinsic qualities of the human 'races' were the order of the day, with clear political and geopolitical implications, amongst them the imperialism of the European powers, particularly Britain, France, and above all Germany, recently risen to the position of a first-rate power.

In Brazil, inevitably, the terms 'race', 'people' and 'nation' formed an almost inescapable part of the vocabulary of the political discussion of the time. Many intellectuals asked themselves how the country could achieve progress and

---

[9] The scientistic creed was strong in Western thinking at the time, even though criticism of positivism and naturalism at the end of the nineteenth century had been bruising, as can be seen from the thought of Dilthey, Nietzsche and, a little later, Bergson.
[10] See Ventura, op. cit.
[11] Lilia Moritz Schwarcz, *O espetáculo das raças: cientistas, instituições e questão racial no Brasil, 1870–1930* (São Paulo: Companhia da Letras, 1993), pp. 43–66.
[12] Arthur de Gobineau (1816–1882), a French diplomat who served in Rio de Janeiro, wrote an *Essai sur L'Inégalité des races humaines* (1853–55), in which he criticized miscegenation between the 'races', and cited Brazil as a negative example. Louis Agassiz (1807–1873), a Swiss national who became a professor at Harvard University, visited Brazil, as a result of which he wrote his *Journey in Brazil* (1867), in which he defended the notion of the purity of the 'white race', identifying Brazilian miscegenation as something to be avoided.

civilization with the population it had. Obviously the responses were varied, but it one way or another it was almost impossible to avoid discussing the black population, miscegenation, and European immigration.[13]

Amongst the consequences of this cultural world, as has been indicated, may be noted the remarkable increase in European immigration to Brazil.[14] At this time many scholars and commentators, among them Sílvio Romero, believed in whitening the Brazilian population, both ethnically and culturally, by way of a Westernizing of the way of life and of social and economic organization.

★ ★ ★ ★ ★

Sílvio Romero was an intellectual typical of the generation of 1870. He wrote a book, *História da literatura brasileira* (1888), that was complex, contradictory and very concerned to understand Brazil, and still considered today his most important work. In his book he attempted not just to recount the history of the country's literature but to tell the story of Brazil. His scientism, so characteristic of his generation, did not prevent the creation of an interpretative vision of Brazilian society, frankly inspired by nationalist ideas, as he confesses in the very first pages:

> Se me faltou o talento, resta-me, em todo o caso, a face moral da empresa; a verdade e o patriotismo foram meus guias [...]. Independência literária, independência científica, reforço da independência política do Brasil, eis o sonho de minha vida! Sejam eles a tríplice empresa do futuro. Tenhamos confiança![15]
>
> [If I have been lacking in talent, I am left, in any case, with the moral aspect of the undertaking; truth and patriotism have been my guides [...]. Literary independence, scientific independence, a strengthening of the political independence of Brazil, this is the dream of my life! Let these be the three-fold undertaking of the future. Let us have confidence!]

The work is a treatise, intended to make the country leap out of its pages. As one of the most important sociological works written at the end of the nineteenth century, his *História da literatura brasileira* was the first systematic and all-embracing attempt to historicize the country's literature, and to see it as the fruit of the society that produced it. Some of the most respected readers of Romero's work, notably Antônio Cândido, Sérgio Buarque de Holanda,

---

[13] Apart from Machado de Assis, as we shall see later, Manuel Bomfim, in his book *América Latina: males de origem* (1905), was one of the few intellectuals to dismiss 'race' as a problem, preferring to examine the Iberian colonial past, its disdain for education and science, and the elitist and formalist mentality of the Ibero-American elites.

[14] Although the figures are contested, it is estimated that between 1882 and 1934 approximately 4.5 million immigrants entered the country, almost entirely European, and principally Portuguese, Italian, Spanish and German. Some of these immigrants returned to their country of origin or migrated to other countries such as Argentina. However, more than two-thirds of this human force remained in Brazil.

[15] Romero, *História da literatura brasileira*, I, 48.

José Guilherme Merquior and Roberto Ventura, agree in their judgement that his work is, before anything else, a treatise on Brazilian culture and society. His great obsession was to explain the country, rather than its literature as such. Romero's sympathies did not engage with the subtle intricacies of the literature, nor with questions relating to language; it was an interpretation of Brazil that truly motivated him, as José Guilherme Merquior has noted:

> Os juízos estéticos de Sílvio Romero são às vezes claudicantes, às vezes insustentáveis (por exemplo o endeusamento de Tobias — dado por superior a Castro Alves... — a subestimação parcialíssima de Machado de Assis); contudo, o estilo ágil e combativo facilita a leitura, e o patriotismo sem ufanismo faz desse colosso historiográfico, ao qual se deve a fixação definitiva (em termos globais) do nosso corpus literário, um depoimento fundamental sobre o itinerário da cultura brasileira.[16]

> [Sílvio Romero's aesthetic judgements are at times wavering, at times unsustainable (for example his lionizing of Tobias — taken as superior to Castro Alves — and his very biased underestimation of Machado de Assis); however, his nimble and combative style facilitates reading, and his patriotism, without chauvinism, makes this monument of historiography — to which we owe (in broad terms) the definitive establishment of our literary corpus — into a fundamental record of the itinerary of Brazilian literature.]

Sérgio Buarque de Holanda seems to confirm the notion that both the wealth and the poverty of the critic reside in his sociological perspective. It is there that may be found the interpretative zeal and the militant dedication that drove him to write the *História da literatura brasileira*, in which he developed an 'ambitious programme', devoted to a detached reading of the texts that made up the literary tradition of the country (apart from its popular tradition), with the aim of capturing the 'generality' of Brazil:

> Inscrevendo a atitude literária e intelectual numa portentosa construção, que tinha por ápice a sociologia, ele desdenhou constantemente a atitude daqueles que, como José Veríssimo, por exemplo, se teriam preocupado em 'obedecer, no estudo dos autores, ao critério puramente estético'. Para ele, as criações da inteligência e da imaginação eram partes integrantes de um todo, e nada representavam quando destacadas dele. Por isso mesmo convinha considerar, nestas criações, e principalmente através delas, o meio, as raças, o folclore, as tradições do país. E foi esse, em suma, o programa ambicioso que ele traçou para a elaboração de sua obra mestra.[17]

> [By placing his literary and intellectual approach within an imposing edifice which had at its apex sociology he always disdained the approach of those, such as José Veríssimo, for example, who were preoccupied with

---

[16] José Guilherme Merquior, *De Anchieta a Euclides: breve história da literatura brasileira* (Rio de Janeiro: José Olympio, 1977), p. 112.
[17] Sérgio Buarque de Holanda, *O espírito e a letra: estudos de crítica literária*, 2 vols (São Paulo: Companhia das Letras, 1996), II, 363.

'following, in their study of authors, purely aesthetic criteria'. To him, the products of intelligence and imagination were integral parts of a whole, and represented nothing when detached from them. For that very reason, it was necessary to pay regard within these works, and particularly through them, to the environment, the races, folklore, and the traditions of the country. And this was, in short, the ambitious programme he outlined for the making of his masterpiece.]

He always had his limits as a literary critic, averse to aesthetic considerations, restricting himself to the documentary aspects of literature, and seeing them as a way of accessing society and nationality.[18] He became famous for regarding Tobias Barreto superior to Machado de Assis, as we shall see. But even here he was driven by non-literary considerations. In order to criticize the 'false cosmopolitanism of Rua do Ouvidor', Romero chose to attack Machado de Assis. Despite living in Rio de Janeiro and fulfilling important cultural roles, he never felt at ease in the capital, describing himself as 'a man from the North'.[19]

Sílvio Romero wanted to understand Brazil through its literature, and good literature should tell of Brazil, its peoples and its history. A literary text, therefore, should give expression to a society, a culture and a nation. The ethnological, ecological, social and historical conditions provided the key to understanding how the literary personality had been moulded. The same premise applied also to the philosopher, the scientist or the artist, creating a whole which reflected society.

Romero did not see a direct correspondence between 'evolution' and 'spiritual culture', but at the same time the laws of nature would have an influence, establishing limits imposed by general, impersonal laws — it was here that his scientism lay. His intention was to discover the real Brazil, and its national individuality, through texts, which should reflect the country. With the help of non-literary criteria, by way of 'general laws', the life of the nation and its

---

[18] See Cândido, *O método crítico*, and his *Sílvio Romero: teoria, crítica e história literária* (São Paulo: Edusp, 1978). Also, Luis Costa Lima, *Dispersa demanda* (Rio de Janeiro: Francisco Alves, 1981).

[19] Sílvio Romero was born in Sergipe, in the Northeast of Brazil, and studied in the Faculty of Law, in Recife, in the neighbouring province of Pernambuco. He spent the greater part of his adult life in Rio de Janeiro. However, he always considered himself a 'man from the North', as the Northeast was known at the time. The author became a federal deputy, representing Sergipe, for a short time (1900–02). He came from a family of landowners, though already in economic decline. For men like him, who had received the best education in Brazil for his time, writing represented one the few careers that could guarantee prestige and recognition. Though he came from a white family of patrician origin, Romero lived modestly off his teacher's salary and from the money he received for his books and journalism. It was probably for this reason that he never felt himself to be a full member of Rio de Janeiro's urban elite, at which he directed harsh criticisms. Machado de Assis, from Rio, though a mulato and of humble origins, was able to obtain important public positions, and unlike Romero, mixed with the Brazilian elite of the time.

people would be — or should be — silently deposited in the country's literary archive. The 'spiritual creations', therefore, would conform to historical and natural factors, and as a result it made no sense for them to be based exclusively on foreign works, since they had been produced under other conditions; hence the need for a literature that would allow 'our national character' to emerge:

> Pretendo escrever um trabalho naturalista sobre a história da literatura brasileira. Munido do critério popular e étnico para explicar o nosso caráter nacional, não esquecerei o critério positivo e evolucionista da nova filosofia social, quando tratar de notar as relações do Brasil com a humanidade em geral.
> Nós os brasileiros não pensamos ainda muito, por certo, no todo da evolução universal do homem; ainda não demos um impulso à direção geral das ideias, mas um povo que se forma não deve só pedir lições aos outros, deve procurar ser-lhes também um exemplo. [...]
> Esta obra contém duas partes bem distintas; no primeiro livro indicam-se os elementos de uma história natural de nossas letras; estudam-se as condições de nosso determinismo literário, as aplicações da geologia e da biologia, as criações do espírito.[20]

> [I aim to write a naturalist work on the history of Brazilian literature. While armed with a popular and ethnic criterion to explain our national character, I shall not forget the positivist and evolutionist criterion of the new social philosophy when trying to define the relations of Brazil with humanity in general.
> We Brazilians still do not give much thought, certainly, to the worldwide evolution of man as a whole; we have still not had an impact on the general direction of ideas, but a people in formation should not only seek lessons from others, it should also attempt to be an example to them. [...]
> This work has two distinct parts; in the first book are sketched out the elements of a natural history of our literature; the conditions of our literary determinism are studied, the influence of geology and biology, our spiritual creations.]

It was armed with this intellectual tool, or rather this view of the world, that Romero read Machado de Assis. Romero showed an enormous passion as a critic and a taste for public debate, and had a notably political approach, particularly when it came to discussing nationality.

This debate, though, was on the literary agenda of the day, attracting the attention of both writers and critics. At the end of the nineteenth century, literature represented a privileged space for public debate. Despite their relatively small number of readers, in a country where the great majority of the population was illiterate, the newspapers gave significant space to literary debates. In this respect, the literary polemics in which authors engaged were also ways of participating in public debate. Sílvio Romero was, perhaps, the greatest polemicist of his time, and did not spare Machado de Assis, an author who had a particular aversion to polemics and aggressive rhetoric.

---

[20] Romero, *História da literatura brasileira*, I, 58–59.

The Beginnings of the Disagreement

In 1897 Sílvio Romero published his *Machado de Assis: estudo comparativo de literatura brasileira*, an interesting and revealing book that has, however, been regarded as one of the greatest mistakes in Brazilian critical writing — and not without good reason. In it the north-eastern critic attacked the Rio novelist for his attitudes and his use of language, while recognizing his literary merits, particularly in style. Set in the form of an indictment, the text seeks to find the defendant guilty.

Engagement in intellectual polemics, a common practice at the time, made use of a forensic format, as Roberto Ventura has observed: 'a polêmica se apropriava da argumentação jurídica: cada um dos debatedores advogava a sua própria causa, como se estivesse diante de um júri hipotético, formado por um público incumbido de assistir à apresentação e à exposição das partes' [the polemic adopted a juridical form of argument: each of the debaters put forward his own case, as if he were before a notional jury, formed of a public responsible for hearing the speeches and explanations of the parties].[21] One of the most evident aims of Romero's accusation was to challenge the canonical position that Machado had achieved in the intellectual and literary environment of the time. More than any other issue, though, Sílvio Romero sought to criticize an alleged lack of national commitment on Machado's part.

Sílvio Romero wrote his book on Machado de Assis with the aim — as the subtitle *Estudo comparativo de literatura brasileira* [*A Comparative Study in Brazilian Literature*] indicates — of comparing him with his own master, Tobias Barreto, an author whom he thought should occupy a central position in Brazilian intellectual life. In a sense his critique represented less a literary debate, as such, and more a dispute over intellectual, aesthetic and political ideas and priorities. It also implied a regional dispute, since Romero questioned the French influence on the Rio intellectuals gathered around Machado de Assis.

Romero's ambitious proposal for an alteration to the canon resulted in a complete defeat for its author, attracting severe criticism. At the time, Lafaiete Rodrigues Pereira, who had taken Machado's side, declared that 'o objeto do livro é Tobias, é a glorificação do teuto-sergipano.[22] Bem sabia o Sr. Romero que se houvesse dado ao livro a sua verdadeira denominação — Tobias Barreto — não teria leitores' [the object of the book is Tobias, it is the glorification of the Teutonic-Sergipean. Sr. Romero knew very well that if he had called the book by its true name — Tobias Barreto — it would have no readers].[23]

---

[21] Ventura, p. 149.

[22] The expression is ironic, since Tobias Barreto read German authors while the great majority of Brazilian intellectuals were profoundly Francophile, or occasionally Anglophile. Romero too liked to quote German authors, though he probably read them in French translation.

[23] Lafaiete Rodrigues Pereira, *Vindiciae: o Sr. Sílvio Romero crítico e filósofo*, quoted in:

In attacking Machado de Assis, Sílvio Romero was targeting, amongst other things, the central position occupied by Rio in the Brazilian intellectual scene, which, as he used to say, emulated the oligarchic spirit of the country's political elite. According to this account, Machado de Assis exercised 'a sort of dynastic policy' in literature.[24] Romero was bothered by the behaviour of Machado, directed to the formation of supportive groups amongst which he evidently played the leading role.

Brito Broca, a long-standing observer of the Brazilian literary scene, considered that 'uma atitude objetiva e imparcial leva a reconhecer no autor de *Dom Casmurro* a mais viva tendência para as "capelinhas" entre nós' [an objective and impartial view leads one to recognize in the author of *Dom Casmurro* the keenest tendency towards 'cliques' amongst us].[25] According to Sílvio Romero, the 'capelinha fluminense' [Rio clique], to which Machado de Assis, José Veríssimo and Joaquim Nabuco belonged, had been particularly unfriendly towards him.

Before resuming discussion of the profound divergence between the two authors, we should remark on the severe criticism that Machado de Assis directed against the young Sílvio Romero. In his article, 'A nova geração', originally published in the *Revista Brasileira*, in 1879, Machado de Assis — who at this time had not adopted the attitude of Conselheiro Aires, with this 'tédio a controvérsia' [weariness with controversy][26] — vigorously attacked the 'moços' [youths], amongst them Sílvio Romero, who in 1869, at the age of nineteen, had published a book of poems entitled *Cantos do fim do século*.[27] The young author's poetry, infected with scientism and doctrinal considerations, was harshly criticized by Machado de Assis:

> Os *Cantos do fim do século* podem ser também documentos de aplicação, mas não dão a conhecer um poeta; e para dizer tudo numa só palavra, o Sr. Romero não possui a forma poética. [...] No livro do Sr. Romero achamos essa luta entre o pensamento que busca romper o cérebro, e a forma que não lhe acode ou só lhe acode reversa e obscura: o que dá a impressão de um estrangeiro que apenas balbucia a língua nacional.[28]
>
> [The *Cantos do fim do século* may also be evidence of diligence, but they do not reveal a poet; and to put it in a word, Sr. Romero does not possess

---

Patrícia Pina (ed.), *Vindiciae: em defesa de Machado de Assis. Polêmica e crítica*, Cadernos da Pós/Letras, 20 (Rio de Janeiro: UERJ, 1998), p. 29.
[24] Sílvio Romero, *Machado de Assis: estudo comparativo* (Campinas: Ed. da Unicamp, 1992), p. 117.
[25] Brito Broca, 'As "capelinhas" literárias', in *Teatro das letras* (Campinas: Ed. da Unicamp, 1993), p. 15.
[26] Machado de Assis, *Memorial de Aires*, in *Obra completa* (Rio de Janeiro: Nova Aguilar, 1994), vol. II.
[27] Sílvio Romero, *Cantos do fim do século* (Rio de Janeiro: Tipografia Fluminense, 1878).
[28] Machado de Assis, 'A nova geração', in *Obra Completa* (Rio de Janeiro: Nova Aguilar, 1994), III, 815.

the poetic mould. [...] In Sr. Romero's book we find that conflict in his thinking that threatens to burst the brain, and the mould that does not suit him, or only suits him contrarily and indistinctly: which gives the impression of a foreigner who merely babbles our national language.]

Sílvio Romero never returned to writing verse, nor did he forget the harsh criticism. In 1885, in an article entitled *Sobre Émile Zola*, he took the opportunity to accuse his opponent of being a sort of late manifestation of Romanticism.[29] However, it was not until his *Machado de Assis: um estudo comparativo*, of 1897, that he settled accounts with him. In one of the passages best-known and most quoted — precisely for being wide of the mark — Romero accuses Machado's language of 'tartamudear' [stammering] and of failing to have great originality. There was in the writing of Machado de Assis, he said, a stuttering which well reflected a spirit that was weak and alien to the social struggle, a spirit characteristic of the author.

> O estilo de Machado de Assis, sem ter grande originalidade, sem ser notado por um forte cunho pessoal, é a fotografia exata do seu espírito, de sua índole psicológica indecisa. [...] Vê-se que ele apalpa e tropeça, que sofre de uma perturbação qualquer nos órgãos da palavra. Sente-se o esforço, a luta. [...]
>
> De fato, Machado de Assis repisa, repete, torce, retorce, tanto suas ideias e as palavras que as vestem, que deixa-nos a impressão dum perpétuo tartamudear.[30]
>
> [The style of Machado de Assis, while not having great originality, not being marked by a strong personal stamp, is an exact photograph of his spirit, of his indecisive psychological nature. [...] We see that he fumbles and stumbles, that he suffers from some disturbance of his speech organs. One senses his effort, the struggle. [...]
>
> In fact, Machado de Assis reconsiders, repeats, twists and turns over his ideas and the words in which he clothes them so much that he leaves us with the impression of a perpetual stammering.]

Wounded pride had surely increased his hostility towards Machado de Assis.

Disputes between intellectual groups are important factors in the formation of the intellectual landscape.[31] However, to reduce the differences to personal resentments or to struggles for visibility and prestige does not explain them, since the disagreements here were really much more profound.

The work of Machado de Assis quite simply does not fit into the interpretative system adopted — and to a certain extent developed — by Sílvio Romero.[32]

---

[29] Sílvio Romero, 'Sobre Émile Zola', in Cândido, *Sílvio Romero*.
[30] Romero, *Machado de Assis*, p. 122.
[31] Pierre Bourdieu, *A economia das trocas simbólicas* (São Paulo: Perspectiva, 1974), p. 99–181.
[32] In *Sílvio Romero, hermeneuta do Brasil* (São Paulo: Annablume, 2005), I examined the assumptions that led the author to construct a 'theory of Brazil', in which miscegenation took the primary place — taken in a certain way positively, despite his belief in the

Machado de Assis was a much greater problem for him than just the critic of his first and insignificant book of poems, which Romero himself later disowned. He was fully aware of Machado's literary qualities. After transcribing the whole of chapter VII of *Memórias póstumas de Brás Cubas*, 'O delírio', he commented:

> Belo, realmente muito belo, como linguagem e estilo. É sem dúvida uma das páginas mais intensas da língua portuguesa. Nem Vieira, nem Herculano, nem Camilo, nem Eça, nem Rui, possuem muitas que a possam ultrapassar. Por amor dela, era caso de estar quase arrependido de tudo quanto, mais ou menos desfavorável, tenho dito em todo o correr deste livro a respeito do romancista fluminense.[33]

> [Fine, really very fine, for language and style. It is without doubt one of the most intense pages in the Portuguese language. Neither Vieira, nor Herculano, nor Camilo, nor Eça, nor Rui have many that could surpass it. For the love of it I almost regret everything, more or less unfavourable, that I have been saying along the whole course of this book about the Rio novelist.]

Sílvio Romero insisted on praising Machado's style: 'parece que honro Machado de Assis, quero dizer, rendo-lhe a homenagem de que é merecedor, como príncipe do estilo entre nós' [it seems that I honour Machado de Assis, I mean, by paying him the homage he deserves, as the prince of style among us].[34] The praise, though, is a criticism, since it reveals the terrain of Romero's unease. What hurt him was Machado's apparent indifference to Brazilian matters. His weariness with political engagement — a stance that Romero regarded as essential to overcome the country's backwardness — as well as the monarchist Machado's apparent conformity to the status quo, formed an accumulation of ideas and perceptions that were contrary to Romero's political sensibilities.

The Basis of the Disagreement

Sílvio Romero strongly identified himself with the modernist generation of 1870, who had taken upon themselves the mission of modernizing Brazilian society in relation to what was happening in the Western world. In their own view, to act in this way would be a way of being open to the future, in harmony with standards in force in western Europe in the second half of the twentieth century.

On the occasion of the admission of Euclides da Cunha into the Brazilian Academy of Letters, in 1906, Sílvio Romero recalled the novelty that the

superiority of the white man. Unlike European intellectuals, such as Arthur de Gobineau, Romero saw miscegenation as being a favourable factor for Brazil. He devoted a large part of his *História da literatura brasileira*, divided into four volumes, to the social, historical and ethnic factors which formed the country.

[33] Romero, *Machado de Assis*, p. 284.
[34] Ibid, p. 129.

scientistic ideology represented. The 'new ideas' seemed to him an investment in the future, a break with what was old and backward, symbolized by the monarchy, by slavery, and by Romanticism. To join forces with the 'party of new ideas' was modern and progressive.

> Até 1868 o catolicismo reinante não tinha sofrido nestas plagas o mais leve abalo; a filosofia espiritualista, católica, eclética a mais insignificante oposição; a autoridade das instituições monárquicas o menor ataque sério por qualquer classe do povo; a instituição servil e os direitos tradicionais do aristocratismo prático dos grandes proprietários a mais indireta opugnação; o romantismo, com seus doces, enganosos e encantadores cismares, a mais apagada desavença. [...]
> Um bando de ideias novas esvoaçou sobre nós de todos os pontos do horizonte. [...] Positivismo, evolucionismo, cientificismo na poesia e no romance, folk-lore, novos processos de crítica e história literária, transformação da instituição do direito e da política, tudo então se agitou e o brado de alarma partiu da escola do Recife.[35]

> [Until 1868, the dominant Catholicism had not suffered the slightest disturbance in these areas; nor spiritualist, Catholic and eclectic philosophy the most insignificant opposition; nor the authority of monarchist institutions the slightest serious attack from any popular social class; nor the servile institution and the traditional rights of the practical aristocracy of the great landowners the most indirect contestation; Romanticism, with its sweet, misleading and enchanting caprices the most discreet dissension. [...]
> A party of new ideas has swept over us from all points of the horizon. [...] Positivism, evolutionism, scientism in poetry and in the novel, folklore, new methods of criticism and literary history, a transformation of the institution of law and of politics — everything then was in turmoil and the cry of alarm was heard from the school of Recife.]

Apart from the infusion of modernity envisaged by these speeches, there was another interpretative pillar that was dear to Sílvio Romero and Euclides da Cunha: a profound national commitment. One may state, in a way, that this commitment personified Romero's intellectual ideal, by its nationalist colouring, and also by its acceptance of science as the interpretative instrument of Brazilian reality. A national engagement and a scientific spirit form the two great pillars of his interpretative system.

Over the nineteenth century, Western culture established a striking linkage between literature and nationalism, a link bred in the womb of the Romantic ideology of the late eighteenth century. The intellectual and artistic environment was fundamental in the construction of a nationalist sensibility, giving literature, historiography and the search for popular traditions a decisive role in the invention of nations.[36] Sílvio Romero respected that tradition, and

---

[35] Sílvio Romero, 'Academia Brasileira de Letras', in *Discursos* (Porto: Lello & Irmão Editores, 1904), pp. 358–60.
[36] See Anne-Marie Thiesse, *A criação das identidades nacionais* (Lisbon: Temas e Debates,

demanded of Brazilian literature that it identify with the nation. Brazil seemed to him to be the undeniable heir of the three races 'atiradas ao cadinho do Novo Mundo' [cast into the melting pot of the New World]. It fell to the intellectuals and writers to uncover and document the identity of that 'povo novo' [new people], child of America and of miscegenation.

> A literatura brasileira, como todas as literaturas do mundo, deve ser a expressão positiva do estado emocional das ideias e dos sentimentos de um povo. Ora, nosso povo não é o índio, não é o negro, não é o português; é antes a soma de todas estas parcelas atiradas ao cadinho do Novo Mundo. São as gerações crioulas, que, deixadas de parte as nostalgias dos progenitores, esqueceram-se delas para amar este país e trabalhar na formação de uma pátria nova.[37]

> [Brazilian literature, like all the world's literatures, should be the positive expression of the emotional state of the ideas and sentiments of a people. Now, our people is not Indian, nor is it Negro, nor is it Portuguese; it is rather a sum of all these parts, cast into the melting pot of the New World.
> They are the native-born generations, which, setting aside nostalgia for their progenitors, have forgotten them in order to love this country and to work for the formation of a new fatherland.]

Machado de Assis, unlike Sílvio Romero, ignored both the nationalist engagement and the militant modernism of the new discourses, evident in realism and naturalism. Machado rejected scientific determinism and even made fun of it in works such as *O alienista* (1882) and *Quincas Borba* (1891). This stance allowed him to avoid writing about the supposed unsuitability of the tropics or the poor ethnic make-up of part of the Brazilian population. His disdain for these doctrines certainly was not agreeable to Sílvio Romero.[38] To his irritation, the mulatto born into a poor suburb of Rio who had become a famous writer neither condemned nor defended miscegenation, nor did he write vibrant pages on the great dramas of the nation, such as the formation of nationality, as the author of the *História da literatura brasileira* would have liked.

Sílvio Romero found himself obliged to live with the accusation that he had not understood Machado de Assis's writings. However, one could take exactly the opposite view. Had not Romero correctly identified in Machado

---

2000); Eric Hobsbawm and Terence Ranger, *A invenção das tradições* (Rio de Janeiro: Paz e Terra, 1984).

[37] Romero, *História da literatura brasileira*, II, 412.

[38] It is interesting to note what Sílvio Romero had read. He considered himself a 'Spencerian liberal', apropos Herbert Spencer. In his *História da literatura brasileira* there are a number of quotations from Ernest Renan, Hippolyte Taine, and from German Romantics, such the Grimm brothers and Johann Gottfried von Herder. Towards the end of his life there are many references to French authors, now completely forgotten, such as Frédéric Le-Play and Edmond Demolins. Space does not permit further development of this question, but the following are recommended: Cândido, *O método crítico*, Ventura, *O estilo tropical*, and Schneider, *Sílvio Romero, hermeneuta do Brasil*.

a powerful if tacit adversary of the nationalist and scientistic ideas that he himself had adopted? The work of Machado de Assis had become a serious problem for Sílvio Romero: he could not ignore it because of the prestige its author had achieved, nor could he simply accept it, on pain of compromising his own intellectual framework. He was committed to forming a systematic interpretation of Brazil, capable of creating durable ideas, such as that of Brazil being a definitively *mestiço* nation — something that still resonates today.

Even if he did not have any great passion for literature, Sílvio Romero was not ignorant on the subject either. In line with intellectuals such as Hippolyte Taine (1828–1893) and Ernest Renan (1823–1892), Romero aimed to examine and document the formation of the nation through its literature, so that writings should serve as evidence. In other words, aesthetic value and language were not at the centre of his concerns. He was less interested in the specificity of the writer and more concerned with his or her capacity to express the life of the country:

> O meio de evitar estes desacertos díssonos e comprometedores é, repetimos, generalizar: ver o povo, onde de ordinário só se costuma enxergar o indivíduo; tomar a evolução das letras e das artes como uma coisa impessoal, de superior às *coteries* de momento, como espécie expoente da vida nacional, uma função da capacidade espiritual da raça. Olhando desta altura da região das ciências, letras e artes, não deixa ela ver os rancorosos conflitos do egoísmo, a pequenez dos temperamentos, o lado passageiro das paixões, para só descortinar aos olhos do observador os grandes, os nobres esforços da alma do povo para a luz, para a glória, para o belo, para os deslumbramentos do porvir.[39]

> [The way to avoid these incongruous and compromising blunders is, I repeat, to generalize: to see the people where ordinarily only the individual is perceived; to take literature and the arts as something impersonal, superior to the cotteries of the moment, as an interpretative specimen of the national life, a feature of the spiritual capacity of the race. Looking at the areas of the sciences, literature and the arts from this height, allows it to ignore the rancorous conflicts of egotism, the pettiness of temperaments, the passing partiality of passions, to reveal to the eyes of the observer the great and noble strivings of the soul of the people for the light, for glory, for beauty, for the fascination of the future.]

As may be noted, the function of literature in Romero's world was certainly very different to Machado de Assis's appreciation of it. Criticizing Romero in 'A nova geração', Machado had identified as a 'disadvantage' a definition of literature that did not privilege the aesthetic sense, and also, ironically, noted in scientism — understood here as the distinctive mark of an age — a sensibility making way for impersonality.

> Depois de ter refutado todas as teorias, o Sr. Sílvio Romero conclui que a nova intuição literária nada conterá de dogmática — será um resultado

[39] Romero, *História da literatura brasileira*, I, 43.

do espírito geral da crítica contemporânea. Esta definição, que tem a desvantagem de não ser uma definição estética, traz em si uma ideia compreensível, assaz vasta, flexível, adaptável a um tempo em que o espírito recua os seus horizontes.[40]

[Having refuted every theory, Sr. Sílvio Romero concludes that there is no dogmatism in the new literary insight — it results from the general spirit of contemporary criticism. This definition, which has the disadvantage of not being an aesthetic definition, carries within it an understandable idea, quite vast and flexible, and adaptable to a time in which the spirit narrows its horizons.]

The profound sense of nationality which orients Romero's criticism is central to his book *Machado de Assis*. Sílvio Romero notes in Machado's *humour* an affected imitation of English authors, in conflict with the 'character' of the Brazilian people, supposedly more given to 'satire' than to irony. Machado's pessimism and humour, he claimed, found no echo in the Brazilian literary tradition, since they were foreign and artificial: 'o temperamento, a psicologia do notável brasileiro não são os mais próprios para produzir o *humour*, essa particularíssima feição da índole de certos povos' [the temperament, the psychology of the typical Brazilian are not those most suited to produce *humour*, that most particular feature of the make-up of certain peoples].[41]

Unlike the supposedly affected cosmopolitanism of Machado de Assis, Tobias Barreto was said to possess a 'humor compatível com as nossas raças ibero-áfrico-americanas' [humour compatible with our Iberian-African-American races].[42] In referring to Machado's humour, Romero used and highlighted the English word, while employing the Portuguese word in referring to Tobias, to reinforce the national quality of the latter and the supposed foreignness of the former.

Machado de Assis, though, had created a subtle critique of the Brazil of his time, delicately elaborated and capable of criticizing the interests of the Brazilian elite.[43] Sílvio Romero saw in that subtlety a compromise, an 'indecisive' moment between Romanticism in decline and realism and naturalism in the ascent. In *Machado de Assis*, Romero reaffirmed the key elements of his own intellectual work and criticism, and in effect, of his vision of Brazil, while unwittingly revealing his difficulty in placing Machado in the literary canon that he had constructed. Machado de Assis's work did not fit into his interpretative scheme.

O esquecimento só respeita o escritor cuja obra é, num dado momento, o signo representativo da grande alma de um povo, de uma raça ou da humanidade inteira. [...]

---

[40] Machado de Assis, 'A nova geração', pp. 812–13.
[41] Romero, *Machado de Assis*, p. 133.
[42] Ibid, p. 189.
[43] Roberto Schwarz, *Um mestre na periferia do capitalismo* (São Paulo: Duas Cidades, 1991).

> Deve-se prestar, pois, atenção a Machado de Assis, porque ele, até certo ponto, é a documentação de um momento da psique nacional, e não pelas relações de qualquer espécie que, por ventura, possa ter com os pretensos novos, novíssimos, ou noviciíssimos de qualquer gênero. [...]
>
> Machado de Assis é, disse eu, um representante do espírito brasileiro, mas num momento mórbido, indeciso, anuviado, e por um modo incompleto, indireto, e como que a medo.[44]

> [Oblivion only spares an author whose work is, at a given moment, the representative symbol of the great soul of a people, of a race, or of the whole of humanity. [...]
>
> We should pay attention to Machado de Assis, then, because he is, up to a point, the record of a moment in the national psyche, and not on account of the relation of any kind he may possibly have with the new or newest or ultra-new pretensions of any variety. [...]
>
> Machado de Assis is, I have said, a representative of the Brazilian spirit, but at a morbid moment, indecisive, sullen, and in a limited way, roundabout, as if fearful.]

Sílvio Romero considered engagement to be one of the missions of the intellectual, the writer, the artist and the public figure. Machado de Assis, on the contrary, preferred literary production, which in the eyes of his critic seemed to be a great weakness, willingly 'abstentionist', since he would not take part in the great public disputes. For Romero, the virtue of a man of letters would be proven in the 'struggle' for the great causes.

> Não importa isto uma aprovação a certo absenteísmo muito do gosto dos ânimos fracos, que entendem de salvaguardar a própria pureza, fugindo sistematicamente das tentações. É proceder que nunca aplaudiremos. A virtude prova-se no meio da luta. A sociedade não é um convento de monjas. Que grande mérito advém em não se cobrir de pó a quem não sai à liça do combate e deixa-se tranquilamente ficar em doce e sossegado aposento? Devemos todos, homens de letras ou não, interessar-nos pelas pugnas e pelas dores da pátria.[45]

> [This does not amount to approving a certain abstentionism, so much to the taste of weak souls, who aim to safeguard their own purity, by systematically fleeing from temptation. It's a conduct we shall never applaud. Virtue proves itself in the midst of the struggle. Society is not a convent full of nuns. What great merit accrues from not covering yourself in dust for those who don't enter the lists of combat and allow themselves to remain tranquilly in a sweet and unruffled retirement? We should all, men of letters or not, concern ourselves with the contentions and the pains of the fatherland.]

Sílvio Romero read the work of Machado de Assis through his own eyes. That is to say, he interpreted it according to his own intellectual project, whose objective was to reveal the 'character' of the Brazilian people. Good literature

---

[44] Romero, *Machado de Assis*, p. 153.
[45] Ibid., p. 31.

should express the values and the dramas, 'the contentions and the pains of the fatherland'. Not having seen any of this in the author of the *Memórias póstumas de Brás Cubas*, Romero criticized his style, for its lack of 'colour' or 'imaginative force', for its 'hiding' landscape and the tropical environment, and for its lack of descriptions. This 'anaemia', he claimed, contrasted with the vital characteristics of Brazilian literature, with its touches of nature to which the Romantic authors have devoted such attention. Sílvio Romero's method was always more political than conceptual, which made him a good essayist and perhaps an acute observer of Brazilian life, but it limited his literary criticism.

Instead of harping on the critic's errors, it may be more useful and revealing to understand what led to those mistakes. Despite his debatable literary interpretation, Romero could at least understand some of the underlying features in Machado's work, unlike many of his admirers, captivated by his stylistic qualities. He understood Machado de Assis, and that was just why he attacked him. In identifying what he considered the author's deficiencies, the critic was able to grasp the novelty of his work. Amongst Machado's readers of the time, it was Sílvio Romero who drew (critical) attention to what today tend to be considered his literary qualities. João Cezar de Casto Rocha expresses this clearly:

> Por tudo dizer sem rodeios, Sílvio Romero talvez tenha sido o leitor contemporâneo mais agudo de Machado de Assis, porque foi o único que destacou, com ênfase, as qualidades que hoje reconhecemos como tipicamente machadianas. 'Somente' Romero viu nessas características defeitos que comprometeriam o talento que nunca negou ao escritor fluminense [...]: a fragmentação narrativa; a recusa do grandiloquente; a visão de mundo cética; a desconstrução de sistemas filosóficos; a irônica compreensão da formação social brasileira; a tartamudez, ou seja, a escrita de um narrador ébrio, que atravessa o texto ziguezagueando, deixando os leitores do usual romance oitocentista literalmente tontos.[46]

> [To put it bluntly, Sílvio Romero was perhaps the most perceptive contemporary reader of Machado de Assis, because he was the only one who emphatically highlighted the qualities that today we recognize as typically Machadian. 'Only' Romero saw in these characteristics defects that could compromise his talent, which he never denied to the Rio writer [...]: narrative fragmentation; avoidance of grandiloquence; a sceptical view of the world; the deconstruction of philosophical systems; an ironical understanding of the Brazilian social set-up; the stammering, that is, the writing of a inebriated narrator who zigzags his way through the text, leaving the readers of the normal nineteenth-century novel literally dizzy.]

Sílvio Romero understood Machado's work, and realizing that it was entirely out of tune with his deepest convictions he had no alternative but to attack it.

---

[46] João Cezar de Castro Rocha, ' "O ruído das festas" e a fecundidade dos erros: como e por que reler Sílvio Romero', in *Repensando o Brasil com Sílvio Romero* (= *Revista Tempo Brasileiro*, 145 (April–June 2001)), pp. 84–85.

The 'Instinct' of Machado de Assis and the 'Modernity' of Sílvio Romero

Even though he did not gauge himself by nationalist sensibilities, Machado de Assis could not evade such a burning issue. In 1873 he wrote a famous article entitled 'Instinto de nacionalidade'. In this text one can at once see an irreconcilable difference between Machado's perception and Romero's intellectual project. Machado was never scathing or iconoclastic towards the tradition inherited from Brazilian Romanticism, which in the 1870s had found itself under heavy fire from the 'new generation', within the ranks of which fought Sílvio Romero and many other young writers, all united in one cause: the rejection of Indianist Romanticism.

In 'Instinto de nacionalidade', a few discursive aspects still persist from the Romantics, such as a search for 'local colour', although already quite different to the likes of José de Alencar, for example. Machado saw lines of continuity in the young Luso-Brazilian literary tradition, from Santa Rita Durão — pre-Independence, from the eighteenth century — to the Indianism of Gonçalves Dias, that should be included in the 'generation which even now is dawning', despite the differences. In contrast to Sílvio Romero or Euclides da Cunha, Machado de Assis did not read the tradition with the modernist taste for the future, and recognized in Brazilian Romanticism — engaged in narrating Indianist allegories or tropical landscapes — the 'instinct for nationality'.

> Quem examina a atual literatura brasileira reconhece-lhe logo, como primeiro traço, certo instinto de nacionalidade. Poesia, romance, todas as formas literárias do pensamento buscam vestir-se com as cores do país, e não há como negar que semelhante preocupação é sintoma de vitalidade e abono do futuro. As tradições de Gonçalves Dias, Porto Alegre e Magalhães são assim continuadas pela geração já feita e pela que ainda agora madruga, como aqueles que continuaram as de José Basílio da Gama e Santa Rita Durão. Escusado é dizer a vantagem deste universal acordo. Interrogando a vida brasileira e a natureza americana irão dando fisionomia própria ao pensamento nacional.[47]

> [Anyone who examines present-day Brazilian literature will immediately recognize, as its first characteristic, a certain instinct for nationality. Poetry, the novel, all the literary shapes of thought seek to dress themselves in the colours of the country, and there is no denying that such a concern is a symptom of vitality and investment in the future. Thus the traditions of Gonçalves Dias, Porto Alegre and Magalhães are continued by the established generation and by the one still now dawning, like those others who continued the traditions of José Basílio da Gama and Santa Rita Durão. The advantage of this universal agreement goes without saying. Examining Brazilian life and nature in the Americas will give national thinking a physiognomy of it own.]

---

[47] Machado de Assis, 'Instinto de nacionalidade', in *Obra Completa* (Rio de Janeiro: Nova Aguilar, 1994), III, 801.

This acceptance of the Brazilian literary tradition did not prevent Machado de Assis from taking a critical view of Romantic Indianism. In a way he welcomed the Romantic paradigm of nationality, though he did not hesitate to question the unequivocal nature of its judgement, by denying the exclusivity of the indigenous theme, since Brazilian history could not be reduced to the 'life of tribes, long since defeated by civilization'. Machado also rejected the fetishization of the tropics as a necessary source of poetic inspiration and a reference to Brazilian life, but he did not belittle the 'natureza americana, cuja magnificência e esplendor naturalmente desafiam poetas e prosadores' [nature of the Americas, whose magnificence and splendour naturally challenge poets and prose writers].[48] His interpretation was not governed by an absolute negation of tradition along the lines of Sílvio Romero, who identified in the Brazilian Romantic tradition 'a falta de crítica, a paixão da palavrosidade com prejuízo das ideias e um otimismo extravagante sobre os nossos homens e as nossas coisas' [lack of criticism, passion for prolixity to the detriment of ideas, and an extravagant optimism regarding our people and our affairs].[49] Machado, by contrast, refused to endorse the reaction to Indianism of the new generation, which seemed to him simply an 'error'.

> A aparição de Gonçalves Dias chamou a atenção das musas brasileiras para a história e os costumes indianos. [...] A vida das tribos, vencidas há muito pela civilização, foi estudada nas memórias que nos deixaram os cronistas, e interrogadas dos poetas, tirando todos alguma coisa, qual um idílio, qual um canto épico.
> Houve depois uma espécie de reação. Entrou a prevalecer a opinião de que não estava toda a poesia nos costumes semibárbaros anteriores à nossa civilização, o que era verdade — e não tardou o conceito de que nada tinha a poesia com a existência da raça extinta, tão diferente da raça triunfante — , o que me parece um erro.
> É certo que a civilização brasileira não está ligada ao elemento indiano, nem dele recebeu influxo algum; e isto basta para não ir buscar entre as tribos vencidas os títulos da nossa personalidade literária. Mas se isto é verdade, não é menos certo que tudo é matéria de poesia, uma vez que traga as condições do belo ou os elementos de que ele se compõe [...]. Parece-me, entretanto, que, depois das memórias que a este respeito escreveram os senhores Magalhães e Gonçalves Dias, não é lícito arredar o elemento indiano da nossa aplicação intelectual. Erro seria constitui-lo um exclusivo patrimônio da literatura brasileira; erro igual fora certamente a sua absoluta exclusão.[50]
>
> [The appearance of Gonçalves Dias drew the attention of the Brazilian muses to Indian history and customs. [...] The life of tribes long since defeated by civilization was studied in the memoirs that the chroniclers left

---

[48] Ibid, pp. 802–03.
[49] Sílvio Romero, *A literatura e a crítica moderna* (Rio de Janeiro: Imprensa Industrial de João Ferreira Dias, 1880), p. 186.
[50] Machado de Assis, 'Instinto de nacionalidade', p. 810.

to us, and examined by the poets, each drawing something from them, one an idyll, one an epic poem.

There was then a sort of reaction. There started to prevail the opinion that not all that was poetic lay in the semi-barbarous customs that preceded our civilization — which was true. And not far behind came the idea that poetry had nothing to do with the existence of that extinct race, so different to the triumphant race — which seems to me an error.

Brazilian civilization is certainly unconnected with the Indian element, nor did it receive any input from it; and this is enough for us not to go looking amongst the defeated tribes for the foundations of our literary personality. But if this is true, it is no less certain that everything can be material for poetry, since it carries the qualifications for beauty or the elements that comprise it [...]. It seems to me, however, that after the memoirs that Srs. Magalhães and Gonçalves Dias have written on this matter it is not proper to exclude the Indian element from our intellectual attention. It would be an error to take it for an exclusive heritage of Brazilian literature; but its absolute exclusion would certainly be an equal error.]

Machado de Assis did not agree to restricting literature to works that spoke of local — that is, national — matters, because 'everything can be material for poetry, since it carries the qualifications for beauty'. He did not see any problem with literature 'uninterested in the problems of the day or the century, indifferent to their social and philosophical crises'. We note the attention to the internal dimension of a work, which in itself distances him from Sílvio Romero, inattentive or even blind to aesthetic aspects. As for the 'national spirit', Machado proposed the cultivation of 'inner sentiment', capable of turning an author into a 'man of his time and his country'. Without destroying tradition, adopting first a strategy of affirmation and legitimation and later of denial and attenuation, he succeeded in breaking the continuity of the nationalist paradigm constructed by Romantic Indianism, stripping it of its authority as an exclusive line of continuity, though without this representing an iconoclastic attack.[51]

> Não duvido que uma literatura, sobretudo uma literatura nascente, deve principalmente alimentar-se dos assuntos que lhe oferece a sua região; mas não estabeleçamos doutrinas tão absolutas que a empobreçam. O que se deve exigir do escritor antes de tudo, é certo sentimento íntimo, que o torne homem do seu tempo e do seu país, ainda quando trate de assuntos remotos no tempo e no espaço.[52]

> [I do not doubt that a literature, especially an emergent literature, should feed principally on the matters that its own region offers; but let us not set up doctrines so absolute that they impoverish it. What should be demanded of a writer, above all, is a certain inner sentiment, which can make him into a man of his time and his country, even when he is dealing with matters remote in time and space.]

---

[51] João Hernesto Weber, *A nação e o paraíso: a construção da nacionalidade na historiografia literária* (Florianópolis: Ed. da UFSC, 1997), pp. 58–59.

[52] Machado de Assis, Instinto de nacionalidade, p. 804.

In suggesting an 'inner sentiment' as the foundation of the 'instinct of nationality', Machado aimed to detach himself from the Romantic tradition without, by this, signing up to the modernist theses of the turn of the century; this allowed him to prudently distance himself from their ethnic and geographical determinisms, a temptation that few intellectuals of his time were able to resist. Machado's notion of an 'inner sentiment' was sufficiently open and vague to operate as an antidote to the pretensions of scientism. In shunning both the Romantic tradition and the newly arrived concepts, he was able to see the teleological dimension to the new generation's discursive horizon, which seemed to him 'o inverso da tradição bíblica; é o paraíso no fim' [the reverse of the biblical tradition; it is paradise as end-point].[53]

> A nova geração chasqueia às vezes do romantismo. Não podemos exigir da extrema juventude a exata ponderação das coisas. Não há impor a reflexão ao entusiasmo. De outra sorte, essa geração teria advertido que a extinção de um grande movimento literário não importa a condenação formal e absoluta de tudo o que ele afirmou, alguma coisa entra e fica no pecúlio do espírito humano.[54]
>
> [The young generation sometimes sneers at Romanticism. We can't expect from the very young an accurate consideration of matters. There is no imposing reflection on enthusiasm. Otherwise that generation would have acknowledged that the extinction of a great literary movement does not mean the formal and absolute condemnation of all that it stood for; something enters and remains in the store of the human spirit.]

In grasping what was lacking in Brazil as a nation, taking the nations of western Europe as his measure, Romero demanded the engagement of literature and men of letters in the formation of 'organismo político e social forte, original, seguro, capaz de expressar-se, indicando uma rota própria diante das nações contemporâneas' [a strong political and social organism, secure, capable of expressing itself by marking out its own pathway before contemporary nations].[55] Literature should work unequivocally for the construction of a distinctive Brazil, and support modernization and progress. As we can see, Romero was far from the 'inner sentiment' and the 'instinct for nationality' suggested by Machado de Assis — who did not share his essentialist vision of nationality, nor see literature as a political instrument. Romero understood his opposition, noting that Machado 'não é da raça dos humanitários propagandistas e evangelizadores de povos ao gosto de Tolstoi. É, a meu ver, uma espécie de moralista complacente e doce, eivado de certa dose de contida ironia' [does not belong to the race of humanitarian propagandists and popular evangelizers that Tolstoy admired. He is, in my opinion, a kind of complacent and affable moralist, tainted with a certain measure of repressed irony].[56]

---

[53] Ibid., p. 811.
[54] Ibid., p. 810.
[55] Romero, *Machado de Assis*, p. 154.
[56] Ibid, pp. 318–19.

Machado was not an evangelizer for any cause; on the contrary, he never gave his writings a campaigning character to the detriment of its narrative, artistic and personal dimension — which is not to say that he had not produced a fine appreciation of the Brazil of his time. Simply that he did not give in to the temptation of the determinist elements of modern criticism. Machado's great novels seem to fulfil the expectation of his text of 1873, in which he does not avoid sophisticated and subtle considerations of the Brazilian society of his time. However, he focuses his attention on the 'depiction of manners' and a study 'of the characters', as he suggests in his 'Instinto de nacionalidade'.

> Isento por esse lado o romance brasileiro não menos o está de tendências políticas, e geralmente de todas as questões sociais, — o que não digo por fazer elogio, nem ainda censura, mas unicamente para atestar o fato. Esta casta de obras, conserva-se aqui no puro domínio da imaginação desinteressada dos problemas do dia e do século, alheias às crises sociais e filosóficas. Seus principais elementos são, como se disse, a pintura dos costumes, e a luta das paixões, os quadros da natureza, alguma vez o estudo dos sentimentos e dos caracteres.[57]
>
> [Free in this respect, the Brazilian novel is no less so from political tendencies, and in general from all social questions — which I do not say either to praise it or to censure it, but merely to vouch for the fact. This class of works keeps itself here in the pure domain of imagination, unconcerned with the problems of the day or the century, indifferent to their social and philosophical crises. Its principal elements are, as I said, the depiction of manners and the struggle of the passions, the scenes of nature, and sometimes the study of sentiments and character.]

Sílvio Romero could not perhaps forgive Machado for his lack of interest in the triumphs of the modern world, nor his lack of enthusiasm for his country and his preference for irony and the subtlety of a universalist, pessimistic humanism. 'Por tudo dizer sem mais rodeios: Machado de Assis é bom quando faz narrativa sóbria, elegante, lírica dos fatos que inventou ou copiou da realidade; é quase mau quando se mete a filósofo pessimista e a sujeito caprichosamente engraçado' [Not to beat around the bush: Machado de Assis is good when he writes a sober, elegant, lyrical narrative from the facts that he has discovered or copied from nature; he is almost bad when he takes on the role of pessimistic philosopher or capriciously charming fellow]. Brazilian realities demanded not irony, but criticism; its wretchedness sanctioned not *humour*, but satire and alarm. Machado de Assis's literary work not only diverged from Romero's ideas, but severely, if tacitly, criticized them.

---

[57] Machado de Assis, 'Instinto de nacionalidade', pp. 805–06.

Machado de Assis, Heir to La Mancha; Sílvio Romero, Child of the Nineteenth Century

How was it that Machado de Assis, writing on the periphery of the Western world, was able to reject certain analytical categories dear to the last decades of the nineteenth century, such as realism and naturalism, nationalism and scientism? In refuting scientific determinism, Machado created the conditions for avoiding a condemnation of the Negro, Indian and *mestiço* populations, something that even critical and progressive intellectuals, such as Euclides da Cunha, had been unable to do.

To Carlos Fuentes, Machado de Assis had refused to be boxed in by those perceptions hegemonic in Europe in the second half of the nineteenth century, notably realism and naturalism, looking to more distant authors and times. Machado's critical writings[58] indicate connections with Shakespeare, Voltaire, Diderot and Laurence Sterne, but Fuentes highlights the relationship between Machado and the literary tradition derived from Miguel de Cervantes. It was from there, he claimed, that came the formative elements of a critical and creative response, of his scepticism towards progress and modernity, and of his rejection of xenophobia and Eurocentrism.[59]

The Latin American intellectuals of the nineteenth century, Fuentes continues, felt unable to look to the colonial world — or to Iberian traditions on either side of the Atlantic — for the sources that could feed the great obsession of the time: progress. It was a limitation that Romero fully shared. To be Negro or Indian was to be 'barbarous', to be Spanish or Portuguese was to be 'backward'. Novelty, modernity and the most up-to-date civilization came from France, Britain or the United States.

> Había que ser yanque, francés, o británico para ser moderno y para ser, aún más, próspero y civilizado.
>
> Las imitaciones extralógicas de la era independiente creyeran en una civilización Nescafé: podíamos ser instantáneamente modernos excluyendo el pasado, negando la tradición: no hay creación sin tradición que la nutra, como no habra tradición sin creación que la renueve.[60]

---

[58] We do not aim here to deal with Machado's critical work, which is extensive. The following texts have contributed directly or indirectly to the shaping of the argument in this article: Antônio Cândido, 'O esquema de Machado de Assis', in *Vários escritos* (Rio de Janeiro: Ouro sobre o Azul, 2004); Roberto Schwarz, *Um mestre na periferia do capitalismo* (São Paulo: Duas Cidades, 1990); Roberto Schwarz, *Ao vencedor as batatas: forma literária e processo social nos inícios do romance brasileiro* (São Paulo: Duas Cidades, 1977); Abel Barros Baptista, *A formação do nome: duas interrogações sobre Machado de Assis* (Campinas: Ed. da Unicamp, 2003); John Gledson, *Machado de Assis: impostura e realismo* (São Paulo: Companhia das Letras, 1991); Sidney Chalhoub, *Machado de Assis: historiador* (São Paulo: Companhia das Letras, 2003).
[59] Fuentes, p. 9.
[60] Ibid., p. 10.

[One had to be Yankee, French or British to be modern and to be, furthermore, prosperous and civilized.

The illogical imitations of the independent era believed in a Nescafé civilization: we could be instantly modern by excluding the past, denying tradition: there is no creativity without tradition, as there will be no tradition without the creativity that renews it.]

For Sílvio Romero, the colonial past was a central problem, handled in a ambiguous and uneasy way, as was all his work. For him, the essential foundations of nationality had their roots in the colonial period — whence miscegenation, taken by Romero as the kernel of Brazilian nationality — but there too was the origin of the nation's backwardness. In the final analysis the colonial tradition was a burden, since from it came the 'inferior races' and the heavy heritage of slavery.

The Iberian colonizers were treated in a tortuous way, now praised, now defamed. In his *História da literatura brasileira*, Romero devoted himself to defending a new direction for Brazil that could overcome the colonial tradition. Praise for the 'great creative nations' and their alleged entrepreneurial capacity implied an enthusiasm for modern capitalism, which Romero related to the 'Anglo-Germanic nations', the nations which had opened up the 'modern era'; it was there the 'lessons' could be learned, needed to 'correct the Latin deficiencies'.

> O povo brasileiro não pertence ao número das nações inventivas; tem sido, como o português, organicamente incapaz de produzir por si.
>
> Tanto quanto se deve aos povos fracos aconselhar que busquem exemplo nas grandes nações criadoras, eu avisara aos brasileiros das vantagens que lhes pode advir das lições das gentes anglo-germânicas, corrigindo as debilidades latinas.
>
> Tocando em fatos diretos, basta não esquecer que às gentes do norte, tendo hoje a sua frente os ingleses e alemães, está reservado o papel histórico, já vinte vezes cumprido, de tonificar de sangue e ideias os povos latinos, célticos e ibéricos do Meio-Dia.[61]

[The Brazilian people do not belong to the ranks of the inventive nations; they have been, like the Portuguese, organically incapable of producing for themselves.

In as far as it is proper to suggest to the weak nations to look to the great creative nations for an example, I would advise the Brazilians of the advantages they may derive from the lessons of the Anglo-Germanic peoples, for correcting the Latin deficiencies.

To deal with hard facts, it is enough to recall that it is to the people of the north, having today at their head the English and Germans, that is reserved the historic role, already fulfilled twenty times over, of fortifying the blood and the ideas of the Latin, Celtic and Iberian peoples of the South.]

Machado de Assis, a reader of the classical tradition and of English-language

---

[61] Romero, *História da literatura brasileira*, I, 167.

authors — such as Laurence Sterne, who loved Cervantes[62] — may have renewed the tradition of La Mancha, avoiding a doctrinal tone, cultivating humour and doubt, and cherishing the relationship with the reader — for example, by warning him that in his hands were his 'memórias póstumas' [posthumous memoirs], written 'com a pena galhofa e a tinta da melancolia' [with cheery pen and melancholy ink].[63] The passages in which Machado addresses his reader are well-known and frequent; it is a narrative gesture loaded with meaning, insofar as it regards the reader (and thus interpretation) as part of the literary make-up — very different to the attitude of an omnipotent narrator, ready to 'teach'.

Sílvio Romero, on the contrary, addressed the reader in a professional tone, spoke with the authority of science, of the authoritative critic, as holder of the very sovereignty of contemporary knowledge. This was not just a difference in style, but of different functions attributed to the text. Romero's writing was imbued with a mission, engaged, concerned to spur readers to action, which was why he had difficulty, not in understanding Machado's work, but in validating Machado's outlook, which was highly critical towards him — as Romero very well understood.

Romero's aim of explaining Brazil showed a troubled nationalist conscience, oscillating between optimism and pessimism. He examined Brazilian life, and, at the same time, studied European theoreticians, drawing contradictory responses from these viewpoints. The intellectual imagination of the nineteenth century had penetrated deeply into his outlook.

Machado de Assis, by contrast, was less susceptible to the hegemonic discourses, less interested in grand explanatory theories, and more inclined to make a bonfire of the universality of man, with his covert strategies, his calculating generosity, or his ingenuity, the play of appearances, his concealed class interests, with Brazil and Rio de Janeiro of his age being the time and place upon which his gaze fell. Without being hemmed in by national identity, Machado was able to speak of his country and his time, able to affirm and to compare, to criticize and to understand, alluding to Brazilian affairs without falling into either nationalist or anti-nationalist discourses — subtleties impossible to the intellectual and political commitment of Sílvio Romero. Machado's discourse, free of visceral loyalties or 'evangelizing' missions, allowed the Wizard of Cosme Velho to practise a literature which implicitly and tacitly criticized Romero's intellectual constructs at its very foundations, producing absences and silences that sounded strident to the ears of Sílvio Romero.

This article was translated from the Portuguese by Richard Correll

---

[62] In his *Memórias póstumas de Brás Cubas*, Machado de Assis explicitly recognized his debt to Laurence Sterne: 'I adopted Sterne's free manner...'. Machado de Assis, *Memórias póstumas de Brás Cubas* (Rio de Janeiro: Ediouro, 1995), p. 13.
[63] Ibid.

A New Account of the Lisbon Earthquake: Marginalia in Joaquim José Moreira de Mendonça's *Historia Universal dos Terremotos*

MARK MOLESKY

On All Saints Day (1 November) 1755, a powerful earthquake, followed by a terrible tsunami and a savage fire, largely destroyed the capital of the Portuguese Empire. One of the most consequential natural disasters in European history, the Great Lisbon Earthquake would have an impact far beyond its destructive reach. In Portugal, it would produce a new political realignment led by the brutal, yet reform-minded, Marquis de Pombal, while throughout Europe, it would trigger an intense debate about the nature and causes of the event by some of the leading minds of the eighteenth century.[1]

Despite the significance of the disaster, however, the number of Portuguese eyewitness accounts of the earthquake is relatively small. Many of the most dramatic and detailed first-hand reports of the tragedy are found in the letters of foreign residents of Lisbon writing home to family and friends.[2] With several notable exceptions (Figueiredo's *Commentario Latino e Portuguez Sobre*

---

[1] For works on this debate, see Thomas Kendrick, *The Lisbon Earthquake* (London: Methuen, 1956); *O Grande Terramoto de Lisboa: Ficar diferente*, ed. by Helena Carvalhão Buescu and Gonçalo Cordeiro (Lisbon: Gradiva, 2005); *Das Erdbeben von Lissabon und der Katastrophendiskurs im 18. Jahrhundert*, ed. by Gerhard Lauer and Thorsten Unger (Göttingen: Wallstein Verlag, 2008); Jean-Paul Poirier, *Le Tremblement de terre de Lisbonne, 1755* (Paris: Odile Jacob, 2005); *The Lisbon Earthquake of 1755: Representations and Reactions*, ed. by Theodore E. D. Braun and John B. Radner (Oxford: Voltaire Foundation, 2005); *O Terramoto de 1755: Impactos históricos*, ed. by Ana Cristina Araújo, José Luís Cardoso, and Nuno Gonçalo Monteiro (Lisbon: Livros Horizonte, 2007); Ulrich Löffler, *Lissabons Fall — Europas Schrecken* (Berlin: Walter de Gruyter, 1999); Isabel Maria Barreira de Campos, *O Grande Terramoto (1755)* (Lisbon: Parceria, 1998); *1755: Catástrophe, Memória e Arte*, ed. by Helena Carvalhão Buescu, Manuela Carvalho, Fernanda Gil Costa, and João Almeida Flor (Lisbon: Ediçoes Colibri, 2006); Grégory Quenet, *Les Tremblements de terre aux XVII et XVIII siècles: La Naissance d'un risque* (Seyssel, France: Champ Vallon, 2005); and Susan Neiman, *Evil in Modern Thought* (Princeton, NJ: Princeton University Press, 2002).

[2] See *O Terramoto de 1755: Testemunhos Británicos — The Lisbon Earthquake of 1755: British Accounts*, ed. by Judite Nozes (Lisbon: Lisóptima Edições, 1990), Jacome Ratton, *Recordações de Jacome Ratton sobre Ocurrências do seu Tempo em Portugal de Maio de 1747 a Setembro de 1810* (Lisbon: Fenda Edições, 2007) and Arnaldo Pinto Cardoso, 'O Terramoto de Lisboa (1755): Documentos do Arquivo do Vaticano', *Revista de História das Ideias*, 18 (1996), 441–510. See also *O Terrível Terramoto da Cidade que foi Lisboa: Correspondência do Núncio Filippo Acciaiuoli (Arquivos Secretos do Vaticano)*, ed. and trans. by Arnaldo Pinto Cardoso (Lisbon: Alêtheia Editores, 2005).

o Terremoto e o Incendio de Lisboa, Moreira de Mendonça's *Historia Universal dos Terremotos*, Brandão Ivo's *Nova e Fiel Relação que Experimentou Lisboa, e Todo Portugal no 1 de Novembro de 1755*, and Portal's *Historia da Ruina* [...]), relatively few literate *lisboetas* who survived the earthquake felt the need to commit their personal experiences to paper in any extended fashion.³ The reasons for this remain unclear. Perhaps the shared nature of the disaster among survivors (the earthquake was felt throughout Portugal and the tsunami impacted almost the entire Portuguese coastline), as well as the fact that many fled to the homes of relatives across the country, made such communication unnecessary.⁴

This article will translate and comment upon a previously unknown Portuguese eyewitness account of the Lisbon Earthquake written in the margins of a copy of Joaquim José Moreira de Mendonça's *Historia Universal dos Terremotos*, presently held in the Rare Books Division of the New York Public Library.⁵ Rendered in brown ink and a highly legible handwriting consistent with the eighteenth century (including the use of the medial *s*), it provides a brief, but valuable, perspective on all three phases of the Lisbon disaster: the earthquake, the tsunami, and the fire. Although clues in the text point to the author's possible area of residence in Lisbon, the author's name, gender, and profession remain unknown. The probability is high, however, that the marginalia author was male because the overwhelming majority of earthquake eyewitness accounts were written by men. A conspicuous exception is Sister Catherine 'Kitty' Witham, whose letters to her mother and aunt back in Great Britain describe in simple, evocative prose the earthquake's impact on Lisbon's 'English nunnery.'⁶

Published in 1758, three years after the disaster, the *Historia Universal dos Terremotos* is widely recognized as one of the definitive eighteenth-century accounts of the Lisbon earthquake in Portuguese and therefore a suitable place for an eyewitness to insert his or her recollections of the event. Written by Joaquim José Moreira de Mendonça, who was employed by the *Torre do*

---

³ António Pereira de Figueiredo, *Commentario Latino e Portuguez Sobre o Terremoto e o Incendio de Lisboa* (Lisbon: Officina de Miguel Rodrigues, 1756), Joaquim José Moreira de Mendonça, *Historia Universal dos Terremotos* (Lisbon: Antonio Vicente da Silva, 1758), Miguel Tibério Pedegache Brandão Ivo, *Nova e Fiel Relação que Experimentou Lisboa, e Todo Portugal no 1 de Novembro de 1755 Com Algumas Obervações Curiosas, e a Explicação das Suas Causas* (Lisbon: Officina de Manoel Soares, 1756), Fr Manoel Portal, 'Historia da Ruina da Cidade de Lisboa cauzada pello espantozo terremoto e incendio, que reduzio a pó e cinza a melhor, e mayor parte desta infeliz Cidade' (manuscript). The Portal manuscript is quoted extensively in vol. III of Francisco Luiz Pereira de Sousa, *O Terremoto de 1 de Novembro de 1755 em Portugal e um Estudo Demografico*, 4 vols (Lisbon: Tipografia do Comercio, 1919), among others. The original resides in the Archivo Nacional da Torre do Tombo.
⁴ For a more extensive list of eyewitness accounts see the bibliography in Campos's *O Grande Terramoto (1755)*.
⁵ New York Public Library (New York, NY), Rare Books Division, Call #: *KF 1758.
⁶ Quoted in Rose Macaulay, *They Went to Portugal* (London: Jonathan Cape, 1946), pp. 267–72.

Tombo (National Archives) and who experienced the disaster from the Castle promontory overlooking the city, the *Historia* is divided into three sections. Section 1 provides a history of notable earthquakes from antiquity to the middle of the eighteenth century, while Section 2 discusses the Lisbon disaster of 1755, with detailed assessments of the physical losses, including a short account of the author's own experiences. In Section 3, or 'Dissertação Physica', Moreira de Mendonça offers a scientific explanation for the causes of earthquakes.[7] His only other known work is a wedding poem, published eleven years earlier, entitled *Torre de Amor: Epitalâmio às núpcias do senhor Diogo Xavier de Melo Cogominho com a senhora D. Maria Vitória de Morais Moniz de Melo* (Lisbon, 1747).[8]

The NYPL copy of the *Historia* is in almost pristine condition and has its original binding. Although no records exist as to its provenance, a New York Public Library stamp and pencil markings inside the cover (identified by library staff as those of the famous librarian and bibliographer Wilberforce Eames), suggest that it was purchased by the library between 1911 and 1937 (the year Eames joined the Library and the year of his death, respectively). Inside the front cover there is a signature, 'Sarah Jane Hull', possibly from the nineteenth century, as well as a small — and as yet unidentified — coat of arms or *ex libris* image, consisting of a shield with three pieces of pomegranate-like fruit (two fruit separated by a horizontal band from one below). Atop the crest sits a wolf impaled by a spear.

All of the margin notes are found between pages 123 and 139 in Section 2, which concerns the Lisbon Earthquake, and are written in either the side margins or those at the bottom of the page. The notes have been transcribed here in full, as they appear in the text and have not been corrected for spelling or grammar. In every case, a '+' within the body of the text directs the reader's attention to the marginalia, which begin with a similar '+'. The first two annotations, on pages 123 and 127, correctly identify the *Basilica de Santa Maria* as the '*See Velha*' or the 'old Cathedral'.[9]

The first full sentence notation, however, emends a paragraph describing several prominent buildings toppled by the earthquake tremors. After the textual reference 'o [Convento] da Providencia teve grande ruinas; igual calamidade padeceu o Collegio de S. Pedro, e S. Paulo de Inglezes' [The Convent of Providence suffered great destruction; as did the College of St Peter and St Paul], a cross '+' points the reader to an annotation in the margin:

> a Torre cahio, abaixo moreo o Prezedente. (p. 132)
>
> [the tower fell, killing the principal below.]

---

[7] Joaquim José's brother, Verissimo, wrote his own essay on the causes of earthquakes: Verissimo Antonio Moreira de Mendonça, *Dissertação Philosophica sobre o Terremoto de Portugal do Primeiro de Novembro de 1755* (Lisbon: Domingos Rodrigues, 1756).

[8] *Grande Enciclopédia Portuguesa e Brasileira*, 40 vols (Lisbon: Editorial Enciclopédia, Limitada, 1945), XVI, 907.

[9] There is a third such notation on page 141.

The *Colégio de São Pedro e São Paulo*, which is referenced here, was commonly known to residents of Lisbon as the '*Collegio dos Inglesinhos*' [the English College or School].[10] Founded by Dom Pedro Coutinho in 1632 as a seminary for English Catholics, its stated mission was to educate priests who, it was hoped, would return to England 'to comfort Catholics persecuted by the heretics.'[11] If, however, England should one day 'convert to [the] true faith', the college was required to give its income to the *Santa Casa da Misericórdia de Lisboa* [Lisbon's House of Charity].[12] Both Moreira de Mendonça and the French publicist and spy, Ange Goudar, report in their histories that the *Colégio* or 'le Collège des Anglois' suffered terrible physical damage in the earthquake.[13]

Earthquake eyewitness Father Manoel Portal also corroborates the marginalia author's dramatic reference to the death of its principal: 'No Convento dos Inglezinhos cahio a Igreja, e o Convento arruinado e o president ficou morto ao pé da Igreja' [In the English Convent the church collapsed, the convent was destroyed, and the principal was killed at the foot of the church].[14] In a letter to her mother on 27 January 1756, Sister Kitty Witham writes: 'The poor Presedent of the English College was Killd as he was preparing for Mass. tis thought he lived aboute four and twenty hours in the Misery for when they found him he was nowhere Brused by reason he was under a bench.'[15] According to a nineteenth-century guide for British visitors to Lisbon, 'the only Englishman of note who lost his life in the catastrophe was the Rev. J. Manley, President of the English College.'[16] All of this is further corroborated in a passage from the College's annals: 'A parte do Colégio que fica a Este e era a encimada por uma torre com sinos era a única parte que restava do edifício erguido pelo Fundador. Tudo o resto tinha sido deitado abaixo para o novo Colégio. A casa nova resistiu os choques e sofreu pouco, a parte antiga com a torre caíram e aqui o presidente Dr. Manley encontrou uma morte prematura...' [The part of the College which lies to the East and which was topped by a bell tower was the only part remaining of the building erected by the Founder. All the rest had been pulled down to build the new College. The new structure resisted the shocks and suffered little damage, but the old part with the tower fell and here the principal, Dr Manley, met a premature death].[17]

---

[10] Fernando Portugal and Alfredo de Matos, *Lisboa em 1758: Memórias paroquiais de Lisboa* (Lisbon: Coimbra Editora, 1974), p. 200.
[11] Ibid.
[12] Ibid.
[13] Moreira de Mendonça, p. 132. Ange Goudar, *Rélation Historique du Tremblement de Terre survenu à Lisbonne le premier Novembre 1755* (Haye: Chez Philanthrope, 1756), p. 202.
[14] Fr Manoel Portal, *Historia da Ruina...* (manuscript, *Archivo Nacional da Torre do Tombo*), p. 16. Quoted in Francisco Luiz Pereira de Sousa, II, 678.
[15] Macaulay, p. 270.
[16] *The Stranger's Guide in Lisbon or an Historical and Descriptive View of the City of Lisbon and Its Environs* (Lisbon: A. J. P. Calçada do Cabra, 1848), p. 26.
[17] Quoted in Matilde Sousa Franco, *O Colégio de S. Pedro e S. Paulo (dos Inglesinhos) em Lisboa: O renascer de um espaço* (Lisbon: Edição da autora, 1992), p. 13.

Dr Manley's death was particularly worthy of note because he was one of the few prominent persons who died in the disaster.[18] When the earthquake struck on 1 November, many Portuguese noblemen and people of means, etc. were far away from Lisbon, wintering on their country estates. Likewise, a good many of the city's English merchants were also absent. According to the *London Magazine*, since 'insults are frequently offered to Protestant strangers, if met in the streets [on All Saints Day], most of the gentlemen of the English factory go the night before to their country houses, and do not return till the second of November, when everything is quiet. To this unhappy bigotry, which brings many of the country inhabitants to Lisbon to see the show, the great loss of the Portuguese, and, on the other hand, the preservation of the English, is said to be owing.'[19] Unlike many of his countrymen, Dr Manley was a prominent Roman Catholic and thus had no reason to flee Lisbon for the holiday.

The next two annotations supplement Moreira de Mendonça's brief, half-paragraph account of the tsunami of 1 November 1755. They are significant because relatively little is known about the specific physical damage caused by the three great waves that struck Lisbon over the course of fifteen minutes. The '+' marker is inserted after the phrase, 'O impeto das agoas desfez o formosissimo Caes da pedra' [The sudden rush of the water broke up the beautiful Stone Quay]:

> todo se somergiu e aquella praça excepto a escada pelo Oeste ficou pouco appartado de terra tambem o mesmo tempo se somergirão muitas fragatas e alguns fragateiros e nunca mais apparecerão chapios algum nem nada d'elles athe hoje. (p. 134)
>
> [it completely disappeared underwater; and that square, except for the western stairs, was separated a little from the shore; at the same time, many frigates and some crew members disappeared; to this day, no trace of them has reappeared, not even a hat.][20]

A rare occurrence in the Atlantic Ocean, the Lisbon tsunami was triggered by the displacement of water at the earthquake's epicentre, several hundred miles to the southwest of *Cabo de São Vicente* [Cape St Vincent].[21] Its massive waves,

---

[18] The most famous victims were the Spanish ambassador to Portugal, the Count of Peralda, who was crushed in the doorway of his embassy in Lisbon, and the great-grandson of the French playwright Jean Racine, who was swept away by the tsunami as he walked along the isthmus at Cadiz, Spain. Kendrick, pp. 35, 127.

[19] *The London Magazine*, December 1755, p. 587.

[20] '*Se somergiu*' (or *se submergir*) is translated 'disappeared underwater' here instead of 'submerged' because the Stone Quay never resurfaced. '*Chapio*' (or *chapeú*) might also refer to a spindlehead [of a capstan] used on ships.

[21] See Antonio Ribeiro, 'O Sismo de 1755 e o Geodinâmico da Ibéria e Atlântico', in *O Grande Terramoto de Lisboa: 1755*, ed. by Rui Machete, 4 vols (Lisbon: Fundação Luso-Americana para o Desenvolvimento and Público, 2005), I: *Descrições*, pp. 219–36; Carlos Sousa Oliveira, 'Descrição do Terremoto de 1755, Sue Extensão, Causas e Efeitos. O

some as high as fifteen metres, would ravage the northwestern coast of Africa and the western shore of the Iberian Peninsula.[22] Entering the mouth of the Tagus River at approximately 11 a.m., the tsunami crashed into its northern bank three times, causing considerable damage to the coastal areas of Cascais and Belém.[23] Some waves reached five to six metres in height. In Lisbon, the vulnerable, low-lying area along the river, the *Ribeira*, from the *Igreja de S. Paulo* [St Paul's Church] to the *Terreiro do Paço* [Palace Square], suffered the greatest damage.[24] 'In an instant,' recalled an anonymous British resident of Lisbon, 'there appeared at some small distance a vast body of water, rising as it were, like a mountain, it came on foaming and roaring, and rushed towards the shore with such impetuosity that tho' we all immediately ran for our lives as fast as possible [...] many were swept away.'[25] According to one anonymous Portuguese eyewitness, 'more than nine hundred people', who had fled to what they believed to be the safety of the river bank, may have perished as the horrible waves smashed against the shore along the *Terreiro do Paço*.[26]

The most conspicuous non-human victim of the tsunami was the imposing, marble *Cais de Pedra* [Stone Quay] that ran along the *Ribeira* in front of the *Terreiro do Paço*. While it was commonly believed that the *Cais* had fallen into a subterranean cavity, Moreira de Mendonça argues that it was pulled to the bottom of the river by the surging water of the tsunami having first been critically compromised ('*desfez*') by the earthquake.[27] According to him, the military engineers, Carlos Mardel and Eugénio dos Santos de Carvalho, found debris from the *Cais* on the river bed.[28] While the annotator simply refers to

---

Sismo. O Tsunami. O Incêndio.' in same volume, pp. 39–42; Jelle Zeilinga de Boer and Donald Theodore Sanders, *Earthquakes in Human History: The Far-Reaching Effects of Seismic Disruptions* (Princeton, NJ: Princeton University Press, 2005), chapter 5; and M. A. Miranda, P. M. A. Miranda, J. M. Miranda, and L. Mendes Victor, 'Constraints on the Source of the 1755 Lisbon Tsunami Inferred from Numerical Modeling of Historical Data', *Journal of Geodynamics*, 25.2 (1998), 159–74.

[22] See Alexandre Costa et al., *1755 Terramoto no Algarve* (Faro: Centro Ciência Viva do Algarve, 2005), David K. Chester and Olivia K. Chester, 'The Impact of Eighteenth-Century Earthquakes on the Algarve Region, Southern Portugal', *The Geographical Journal*, forthcoming 2010, and Diego Téllez Alarcia, 'El impacto del terremoto de Lisboa en España', in *O Terramoto de 1755: Impactos históricos*, pp. 77–95.

[23] See Olga Bettencourt et al., *Cascais em 1755* (Cascais: Câmara Municipal de Cascais, 2005).

[24] See de Boer and Sanders, p. 94.

[25] Nozes, p. 168.

[26] Letter cited in Pereira de Sousa, III, 539. This number is probably an exaggeration.

[27] See Nozes, p. 170.

[28] Moreira de Mendonça, p. 134. Remains found during the recent construction of the *Terreiro do Paço* metro station are believed to be from the *Cais de Pedra*. See António Correia Mineiro, 'A Propósito das Medidas de Remediação e da Opção Política de Reedificar a Cidade de Lisboa sobre os seus Escombros, após o Sismo de 1 de Novembro de 1755: Reflexões', in Machete, ed., *1755: O Grande Terramoto de Lisboa*, I: *Descrições*, pp. 198–99.

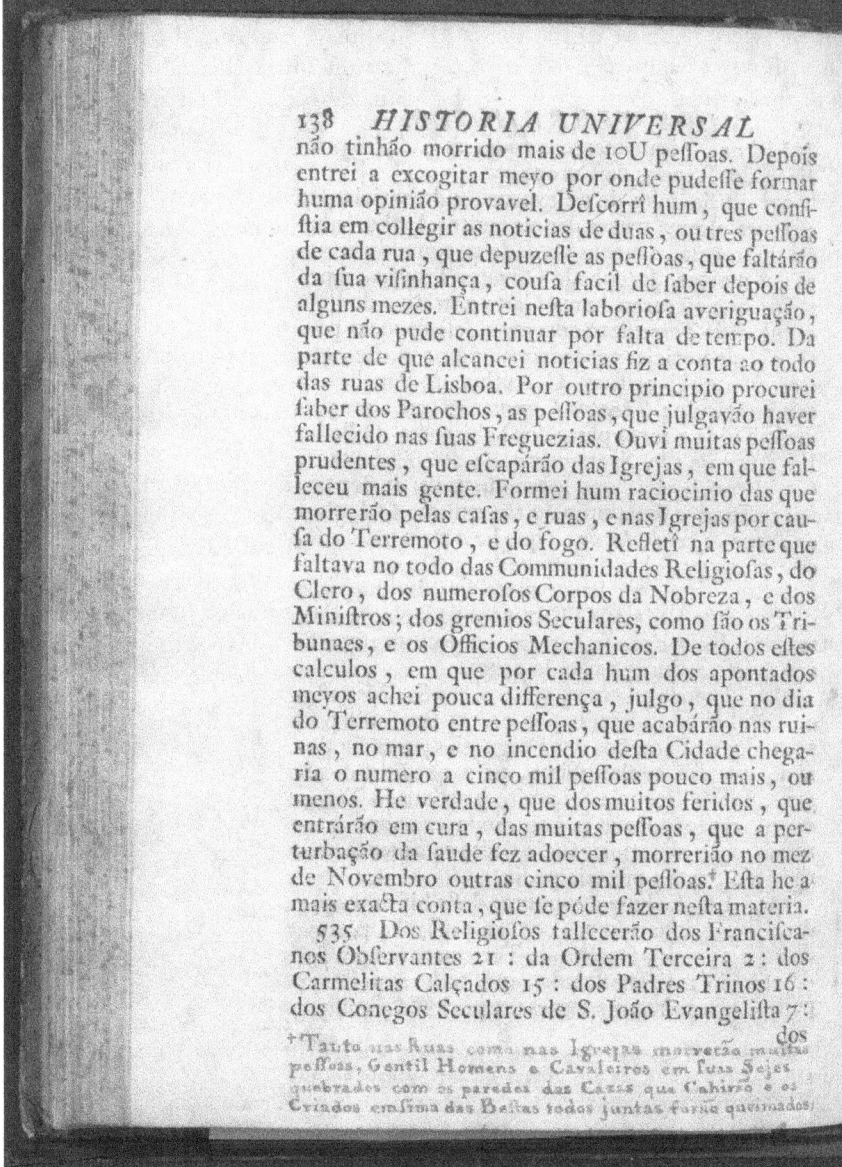

Pages 138 and 139 of a copy of Joaquim José Moreira de Mendonça's *Historia Universal dos Terremotos* (published 1758) held by the New York Public Library, Rare Books Division, call #: *KF 1758. Image provided and reproduced by permission of the New York Public Library.

DOS TERREMOTOS. 139

dos Eremitas de Santo Agoſtinho 5 : dos Dominicos Portuguezes 3 : dos Hibernios 4 : da Companhia de Jeſus 3 : dos de S. Camilo 1 : da Congregação do Oratorio 4 : de N. Senhora das Mercês 1.

536 Das Religioſas Dominicanas morrerão no Moſteiro da Annunciação 10 : no Moſteiro do Salvador 14 : Das Franciſcanas no Moſteiro de Santa Anna 5 : no do Calvario 22 : no de Santa Clara 63. Das Agoſtinhas no Moſteiro de Santa Monica 8.

537 Da Nobreza fallecerão ſómente D. Franciſco de Noronha, filho dos Marquezes de Anjeja, Principal da Santa Igreja Patriarchal; Gaſpar Galvão de Caſtellobranco, e Manoel de Vaſconcellos Gayo, Monſenhores; Manoel Varejão de Tavora, Inquiſidor de Lisboa; Antonio de Mello de Caſtro, Roque de Souſa; Franciſco Luiz da Cunha e Ataide, Chanceller mór do Reyno; e Pedro de Mello de Ataide, Secretario de Guerra. Tambem falleceu D. Bernardo de Rocaberti, Conde de Peralada, Embaxador do Rey Catholico neſta Corte ao ſahir do Palacio, em que morava.

538 Das Senhoras da primeira Nobreza falleceu Dona Maria da Graça de Caſtro, Marqueza de Louriçal; Dona Anna Vicencia de Noronha, Condeſſa de Lumiares com a filha mais velha ; Dona Anna de Moſcoſo, mulher de Gonçalo Xavier de Alcaçova Carneiro ; Dona Iſabel Catharina Henriques, Viuva de D. Lourenço de Almeida, e ſua Filha.

539 Sigo neſtas noticias o doutiſſimo Commentario do Padre Antonio Pereira da Congregação do Oratorio, que as averiguou com exacção, a que ſó fiz algumas addiçoens; cuja obra, ainda que conciſa merece a eſtimação de primeira neſta mate-
S 2 ria

the disappearance of the *Cais*, his detailed account of significant earthquake damage to the *Ribeira* (here and in the next notation) adds credence to Moreira de Mendonça's view. Likewise, the reference here to very specific details, like the condition of the 'western stairs' or the slight separation of the *Terreiro do Paço* from the shore, suggests that the annotator was an eyewitness.

Although the annotator does not mention the many victims were swept away as they took refuge on the *Cais de Pedra* in front of the *Terreiro do Paço*, he does refer to the ships in the Tagus that sank or were pulled out to sea. Wrote one British eyewitness: 'A great number of boats and small vessels, anchored near it, all likewise full of people who had retired thither [...], were swallowed up, as in a whirlpool, and never more appeared.'[29] The remark in the marginalia that no trace of these ships or their crew has reappeared 'to this day' suggests that the annotator was writing relatively close to the event.

The following passage provides more details about the damage to the *Ribeira* by both the earthquake and tsunami.

> Tambem a Cappella e toda aqu'lla parede do Alfandega e toda a parede do Almazem d'aquella banda da praya e toda a parede do Jardim do Tabaco ou Almazem para banda do Caes se somergiu com os Caes de pedra e o grande Circo de Terreiro do passo se somergiu duas polgadas de medida e a terra em muitas partes abriu ainda em algumas abaixou a terra pouco, e o monte sinais abaixou alguma couza. (pp. 135–36)

> [In addition, the chapel and the entire wall of the Customs House and the entire wall of the warehouse facing the beach and the entire wall of the Tobacco Garden or warehouse facing the Quay disappeared underwater along with the Stone Quay; and the great circular enclosure of the Palace Square [*Terreiro do Paço*] was submerged two inches; and in many places the earth opened up and, in others, the earth was lowered a bit, and the hill [showed (deu)] signs of being lowered somewhat.]

According to the annotator, the water swept away the riverside walls of the *Alfândega* (Customs House) and the *Alfândega do Jardim do Tabaco* (Customs House of the Tobacco Garden), leaving approximately two inches of water in the *Terreiro do Paço* after the waves receded.[30] In his *Verdade Vindicada*, José Acursio de Tavares similarly reports that 'o Cais da Pedra inteiramente se abateo com parte do Jardim do tabaco e Alfandega' [the Stone Quay completely shattered along with part of the Tobacco Garden and Customs House].[31] One Spanish eyewitness writing in Italian claims that the water reached all the way to the 'Rue Nuova' (*Rua Nova*), a full block north of the *Terreiro do Paço*, where, he adds, many people were later found 'afogata' [drowned].[32]

---

[29] Nozes, p. 168.

[30] A *polegada* is approximately 2.75 cm, while an inch is 2.54 cm.

[31] Jose Acursion de Tavares, *Verdade Vindicada ou Resposta a Huma Carta escrita de Coimbra, em que se dá noticia do lamentavel successo de Lisboa no dia 1. de 1755* (Lisbon: Miguel Manescal da Costa, 1756), p. 21.

[32] Cardoso, 'O Terramoto de Lisboa (1755)', p. 499.

It seems plausible, therefore, that the tsunami not only breached a portion of an already structurally compromised *Muralha Filipina* (the wall built by Philip II of Spain in the sixteenth century to protect the *Ribeira* from high tides) but washed a portion of it away.³³ This would be a new discovery. In a recent article, António Correia Mineiro contends that the tsunami caused considerably less damage in Lisbon than has previously been believed because the *Muralha Filipina* was not significantly damaged. 'If the wall had collapsed,' he writes, 'it would not have escaped the notice of both contemporaries and historians.'³⁴ While the marginalia passage does not constitute definitive proof of the *Muralha*'s collapse, it does show that the cumulative effects of the earthquake and tsunami caused considerably more destruction in the area of the *Terreiro do Paço* than has previously been reported. Regarding the '*Cappella*' [chapel] it is unclear whether the annotator is referring to the royal chapel of the *Paço da Ribeira* or a hitherto unidentified chapel along the *Ribeira* (perhaps a part of the *Alfândega*).

The hill mentioned in the final phrase of this notation is either the imposing *Monte do Castello* [Castle Hill], which overlooks the *Baixa* from the east and can be seen from the *Terreiro do Paço*, or the *Monte de Santa Catarina* [St Catherine's Hill]. The best evidence for *Santa Catarina* is that the next section refers to three churches that were located on or near it. On its peak sat the imposing *Igreja de Sta. Catharina do Monte Sinai*, named after the fourth-century monastery located at the foot of Mount Sinai in the Holy Land. It is also possible that 'o monte sinais' is a reference to 'Mount Sinai' and that *o Monte de Santa Catarina* was also known at the time as *Monte Sinai* or *Monte Sinais*.³⁵

> E a Igreja de Sta. Catharina quazi toda redunda foy arruinado: e a Igreja da Cruz da Esperança e a Igreja das Inglazinas e muitas outras da mesma sorte em que nellas morrerão muitas pessoas. (p. 137)
>
> [And the Church of Santa Catarina, which was practically overflowing with people, was destroyed: and many people died in the Church of the Cross of Hope and the English Church as well as many other churches.]

Striking at approximately 9:45 a.m. on a Feast Day, when so many were at Mass, the giant earthquake, which registered at least 8.5 on the Richter scale, turned Lisbon's churches into deathtraps.³⁶ That *Santa Catarina* suffered gravely is beyond dispute. Moreira de Mendonça reports that the church was completely destroyed: 'arruinou inteiramente.'³⁷ Agreeing with the annotator

---

³³ As a result of the death of King Sebastian in battle, in 1578, Philip II of Spain took the Portuguese crown in 1580, and remained king until his death in 1598.
³⁴ Mineiro, p. 205.
³⁵ See Maria Calado and Vítor Matias Ferreira, *Lisboa: Freguesia de Santa Catarina (Bairro Alto)* (Lisbon: Contexto Editora, 1992).
³⁶ See António Ribeira, 'O Sismo de 1/11/1755: significado geodinâmico', in Buescu and Cordeiro, pp. 77–86.
³⁷ Moreira de Mendonça, p. 131.

that numerous churchgoers were trapped inside when the tremors began, Fr Portal writes: 'Na Freguesia de S. Catharina aonde e foy baptizado cahio parte do této, e a torre, sepultou muita gente' [In the parish [church] of St Catherine's where I was baptized, part of the roof collapsed along with the tower, burying many people'].[38] One British eyewitness recalls hearing 'the fall of the Parish Church there [on St Catherine's hill], whereby many persons were killed on the spot and others mortally wounded.'[39] In the most celebrated visual depiction of the Lisbon Earthquake — João Glama Stromberle's immense oil painting of the *Praça da Santa Catharina*, now in the *Museu Nacional de Arte Antiga* in Lisbon — the ruins of St Catherine's rise in the background: its roof and tower caved in, its walls scarred with horrible cracks.[40] In the foreground, the wretched survivors hold their heads or gesticulate to the heavens, while priests deliver sermons and give absolution. Was the marginalia author among them?

It is curious that of the three churches mentioned in the margin notes only St Catherine's was a significant Lisbon landmark.[41] Was the annotator reporting the destruction of churches in the neighbourhood where he or she lived? Indeed, St Catherine's, the English College, and the Monastery of Hope were all situated in the southwest corner of Lisbon in the *Bairro Alto* within the parish boundaries of Santa Catarina, Mercés, and Mártires.[42]

The next two passages concern the fire (or fires), which began in several locations throughout the city almost immediately after the first tremor. On this Feast of All Saints, the churches were filled with burning candles and almost every stove in the city was cooking the holiday meal. When the buildings collapsed, the ruins caught fire. Aided by acts of arson (thieves wishing to flush people out of the city to facilitate their plundering), these small fires coalesced into one great blaze — and possibly a firestorm.[43] Of those who were trapped in the rubble, many were burned to death by the rapidly approaching flames. Wrote one British merchant: 'Infinite were the number of broken-limbed persons, who were forced to be deserted even by those who loved them best,

---

[38] Portal. Quoted in Pereira Sousa, III, 37.

[39] Nozes, p. 168.

[40] João Glama Stromberle, *Cena de desolação junto das ruinas da desparecida Igreja de Sta. Catarina ou Alegoria ao Terramoto de 1755 na Cidade de Lisboa* (1760 approx.). See Vítor Serrão, '1755 e as imagens de Lisboa: a *Alegoria ao Terramoto* de João Glama Stromberle', in Buescu and Cordeiro, pp. 191–205. Santa Catarina Square was known as the *bairro* (neighbourhood) of painters in Lisbon. Serrão, p. 204.

[41] The Church of the Cross of Hope is possibly the *Mosteiro da Esperança* (Monastery of Hope), which 'suffered significant damage', according to contemporary church records. *Memórias de uma Cidade Destruida: Testemunhos das Igrejas da Baixa-Chiado* (Lisbon: Alêtheia Editores, 2005), p. 173. '*A igreja padeceu bastante ruína nas abóbadas* [...]'.

[42] The parishes of *Santa Catarina* and *Mercés* were (and remain) contiguous.

[43] See Mark Molesky, 'The Great Fire of Lisbon, 1755', in *Flammable Cities: Urban Conflagration in the Making of the Modern World* [provisional title], ed. by Gregory Bankoff, Uwe Luebken and Jordan Sand (University of Wisconsin, forthcoming).

and left to the miserable torture of being burnt alive.'[44] In the words of one Portuguese priest: 'Abrazarão-se vivas muitas gentes, que não poderão retirar, e muitos que ainda conservavão alentos entre os entulhos, em que estavão' [Many who could not be saved and still drew breath beneath the ruins were consumed alive].[45] Ultimately, the fire would do more material damage than the earthquake and tsunami combined. According to Moreira de Mendonça: 'destruiu o fogo inteiramente os Bairros chamados da Ribeira, da Rua nova, e do Rocio, e grande parte dos Bairros dos Remolares, do Bairro alto, do Limoeiro, e de Alfama, que são os mais ricos, e populosos sete Bairros dos doze, em que se devide a Cidade' [the fire completely destroyed the neighbourhoods of *Ribeira*, *Rua Nova*, and *Rossio*, and the largest parts of the neighbourhoods of *Remolares*, *Bairro Alto*, *Limoeiro*, and *Alfama*, which are the richest and most populous seven neighbourhoods of the twelve that make up the city].[46] One suspects that the marginalia author meant for the following annotation to add colour to a rather dry, analytical passage in which Moreira de Mendonça estimates the total number of deaths in the disaster.[47]

> Tanto nas Ruas como nas Igrejas morrerão muitas pessoas, Gentil Homens e Cavaleiros em suas Sejes quebrados com as paredes das Cazas que Cahirão e os Criados ensima das Bestas todos juntos forão queimados; (p. 138)

> [As many people died in the streets as in the churches, gentlemen and knights in their chaises and servants on beasts of burden were crushed by the walls of falling houses; all were burned together.]

Here, the annotator describes a horrific, yet representative, street scene, echoed by another British survivor: 'We went near two miles through the streets,' he wrote, 'climbing over ruins of churches, houses & stepping over hundreds of dead and dying people, killed by the falling of buildings; carriages, chaises and mules, lying all crushed to pieces.'[48] Indeed, Lisbon's famously narrow alleyways proved so deadly during the earthquake that in the plan for Lisbon's redesign, architects purposely made the avenues wide enough so that

---

[44] Nozes, p. 52.
[45] In Pereira de Sousa, *O Terremoto*, p. 761. A letter from a priest to his brother in Goa (1756), *Instituto da Vasco da Gama*, 46 (October 1875): pp. 238–40.
[46] Moreira de Mendonça, p. 126.
[47] Moreira de Mendonça estimates that five thousand people died as a result of the earthquake, tsunami, and fire on November 1, and another five thousand died of their wounds in the month that followed; p. 138. Some scholars consider these numbers to be too conservative. See Álvaro Pereira, 'The Opportunity of a Disaster: The Economic Impact of the 1755 Earthquake', *Journal of Economic History*, 69.2 (2009), 468–73.
[48] Nozes, p. 148. A chaise is a two-wheeled carriage that seats one or two people. In eighteenth-century Lisbon, it would have been pulled by mules rather than horses, which were reserved for members of the royal court, ambassadors, and foreign ministers. *Travels of the Duke of Chatelet, in Portugal*, ed. by Jean François Bourgoing, 2 vols (London: John Stockdale, 1777), I, 115–16.

collapsing debris would not harm those walking in the centre of the street.[49] By highlighting the fact that the bones of high-born gentlemen were jumbled together and burned with those of servants and animals, the annotator is conveying both the indiscriminate nature of the disaster as well as a typical eighteenth-century sensitivity to class. Indeed, similar sentiments can be found in numerous descriptive and literary accounts of the earthquake. In these lines from a Portuguese poem published in 1756, the levelling power of Nature is presented as both a social and human tragedy:

> General, Sacerdote, Leigo, Frade,
> Cingidos da fatal calamidade;
> Ministro, Pobre, Rico Cavaleiro,
> Commerciante, Soldado, Jornaleiro,
> Miseravel, Felíz, Aborrecido,
> Com todos falla o tremulo gemido,
> A todos vos iguala, a todos peza
> Neste acerbo clamor da Natureza.[50]

> [General, Priest, Layman, Friar,
> Bound together by the deadly calamity;
> Minister, Pauper, Rich Gentleman,
> Merchant, Soldier, Day-Labourer,
> The miserable, the happy, and the weary,
> The trembling groan speaks to everyone;
> They have been made equal;
> This bitter cry of Nature brings unhappiness to all.]

It was this new perception of Nature as capricious and socially blind that may, by undermining confidence in the status quo, have profoundly altered the political landscape of the second half of the eighteenth century.[51]

The following annotation contains another chilling image of the fire's results: charred bones left in the streets and inside buildings.

---

[49] The best book on the rebuilding of Lisbon remains José Augusto França, *Lisboa Pombalina e o Illuminismo* (Lisbon: Bertrand Editora, 1983) (originally published as *Une ville de Lumières, la Lisbonne de Pombal* (Paris: S.E.V.P.E.N. (Impr. nationale), 1965). See also França, *A reconstrução de Lisboa e arquitectura pombalina*, Biblioteca Breve, #12 (Lisbon: ICLP, 1981); John R. Mullin, 'The Reconstruction of Lisbon Following the Earthquake of 1755: A Study in Despotic Planning', *Planning Perspectives*, 7 (1992), 157–79; the articles in *Monumentos: Revista Semestral de Edifícios e Monuments*, 21 (Sept. 2004), Dossiê: 'Baixa Pombalina'; Maria Helena Ribeiro dos Santos, *A Baixa Pombalina: Passado e Futuro* (Lisbon: Horizonte, 2005); and Kenneth Maxwell, 'Lisbon 1755: The Earthquake of 1755 and Urban Recovery under the Marquês de Pombal', in *Out of Ground Zero: Case Studies in Urban Reinvention*, ed. by Joan Ockman (Munich and New York: Prestel, 2002).

[50] Franciso de Pina e de Mello, 'Ao Terremoto do Primeiro do Novembro de 1755: Parènesis de Franciso de Pina e de Mello' (Lisbon: Manoel Soares, 1756), no page numbers.

[51] See Helena Carvalhão Buescu, 'Sobreviver à catátstrofe: Sem tecto, entre ruínas', in Buescu and Cordeiro, pp. 19–72.

os ossos des quais ficarão despois em as ruas junto em aos mesmos apozentos, a vista de qual diu grande medo e horror a todos; em as Cazas morrerão muitos queimados vivas. Durou o fogo na Cidade mais de hum mez. (p. 139)

[The sight of the bones, which remained in the streets and inside homes, was the cause of much fear and horror to all; many people were burned alive in their homes. The fire in the city lasted more than a month.]

Even more than the macabre spectacle, *lisboetas* feared the very real possibility of an outbreak of disease, specifically the plague ('*peste*'). Indeed, one of the first orders given by the king's minister Sebastião José Carvalho e Melo (later the Marquis de Pombal) was for the disposal of the dead, either through burial or by piling the corpses on barges that would be sunk past the Tagus bar in the Atlantic.[52] In 2004, workmen discovered a mass gravesite of earthquake victims beneath the floor of the former *Convento de Nossa Senhora de Jesus* (now the Lisbon Academy of Sciences), revealing bones that suggested 'heavy fire exposure, sometimes with skull opening and splitting'. Other remains displayed evidence of blunt force trauma, possibly from falling objects, and bullet wounds.[53] Undoubtedly one of the difficulties that authorities faced in determining the total number of earthquake victims — beyond the fact that accurate census data was unavailable — was the chaotic, rushed nature of the disposal of the corpses. Moreover, many bodies no doubt disintegrated in the intense heat generated by the enormous blaze.[54]

The final line, which reports that the fire 'lasted more than a month', is most intriguing. While the majority of eyewitnesses say that the blaze lasted between five and nine days, two other sources — the recently discovered letters of Filippo Acciaiuoli, the papal nuncio in Lisbon from 1754 to 1760, and Fr Bento Morganti's *Letter from One Friend to Another* — claim that it continued for at least six weeks. Acciaiuoli's account is particularly useful — and convincing. In attempting to keep Benedict XIV and the Vatican apprised of the tragedy, he provides the closest thing we have to a timeline of the fire — something that is missing in more synthetic accounts. According to the nuncio, on 16 December, six weeks after it began, 'Ancora continua non ispento il fuoco nei sotterranei delle case brusciate e specialmente nei magazzini' [the fire is still not extinguished, it continues in the basements of burned houses and especially

---

[52] See 'Providência I', in *1755: O Grande Terramoto de Lisboa*, ed. by Rui Machete, 4 vols (Lisbon: FLAD and Público, 2005), III: *Providências do Marquês de Pombal*, p. 35.

[53] Miguel Telles Antunes, 'Vítimas do Terramoto de 1755 no Convento de Jesus (Academia das Ciências de Lisboa)', in *e-Terra — Revista Electrónica de Ciências da Terra/Geosciences On-line Journal*, 3, 1 (2006), p. 2. Online at <http://e-terra.geopor.pt/artigos/mta/mta.pdf> [accessed 16 March 2010].

[54] See Neil Hanson, *The Dreadful Judgment: The True Story of the Great Fire of London, 1666* (New York: Doubleday, 2001), pp. 323–33. Hanson speculates that many bodies disintegrated in the intense heat generated by the fire.

stores].⁵⁵ Apparently, the fires continued to feed on a variety of combustible materials (like the slow-burning Brazil wood or *pau brasil*) beneath the rubble. Therefore, it seems plausible that while the main fire lasted perhaps a week, many smaller fires would continue to burn throughout the city for over a month and a half.⁵⁶ After 16 December, Acciaiuoli never mentions the fire again. The Lisbon priest Morganti, however, writes that 'ainda hoje que se contão 19 de Dezembro em muitas partes se conserva fogo' [as of 19 December, the fire continues to burn in many parts [of the city]].⁵⁷ In agreeing with these two eyewitnesses, the marginalia author provides support for a new and more complex understanding of the Lisbon fire. Moreover, by taking an uncommon view on the fire's length — one found in only a single other eighteenth-century source (Acciaiuoli's letters were not published until 1996) — the author, once again, acts more like an eyewitness than a mere chronicler of other accounts.⁵⁸

★ ★ ★ ★ ★

In recent years, scholarly interest in marginalia has grown considerably. In 1998, a conference in Erice, Italy produced two volumes of articles on marginalia in medieval and early modern texts.⁵⁹ In 2001, H. J. Jackson published a general study of the subject with wide multi-disciplinary appeal.⁶⁰ One of the principal concerns of these and other works is how annotations interact with the texts they seek to emend, often adding a competing authorial voice. Unlike most eyewitness accounts of the Lisbon earthquake, the annotations discussed in this article were not intended as a free-standing narrative nor as an overtly personal account, but as a supplement and, in some instances, corrective to Moreira de Mendonça's text. Although an impressively comprehensive catalogue of destruction, the *Historia Universal dos Terremotos* does attempt to downplay the negative legacy of the disaster in several respects. In the first place, Moreira de

---

[55] Cardoso, 'O Terramoto de Lisboa (1755)' p. 465.

[56] At least one fire was still burning in the ruins of the World Trade Center two months after it was destroyed on 11 September 2001. Joachim D. Pleil, William E. Funk, and Stephen M. Rappaport, 'Residual Indoor Contamination from World Trade Center Rubble Fires as Indicated by Polycyclic Aromatic Hydrocarbon Profiles', *Environmental Science and Technology*, 40, 4 (2006), 1172–77.

[57] Bento Morganti, *Carta De Hum Amigo Para Outrao Em que se dá succinta noticia dos effeitos do Terremoto Succedido Em O Primeiro De Novembro de 1755* (Lisbon: Domingos Rodrigues, 1756), p. 4.

[58] Arnaldo Pinto Cardoso 'O Terramoto de Lisboa (1755)', pp. 441–510.

[59] *Talking to the Text: Marginalia from Papyri to Print*. Proceedings of a Conference held at Erice, 26 September to 3 October 1998, as the 12th meeting of the International School for the Study of Written Records, ed. by Vincenzo Fera, Giacomo Ferraù, and Silvia Rizzo, 2 vols (Messina: Università degli studi di Messina, Centro interdipartimentale di studi umanistici, 2002).

[60] H. J. Jackson, *Marginalia: Readers Writing in Books* (New Haven, CT: Yale University Press, 2001).

Mendonça's estimate of 10,000 total earthquake deaths is one of the lowest of any eyewitness.[61] Secondly, his chronicle of earthquakes throughout human history in Section 1 has the effect of making the Lisbon disaster appear less unique.[62] Although no specific evidence exists, it is possible that Moreira de Mendonça was doing the bidding of the Marquês de Pombal and the Portuguese government. In the aftermath of the disaster, Pombal's overriding concern was to project a sense of order and continuity to both foreign powers and business interests, not to wallow in the overwhelming misfortune of his country. Thirdly, Moreira de Mendonça seeks the cause of the earthquake (along with such figures as Miguel Tibério Pedegache Brandão, António Nunes Ribeiro Sanches, and Pombal)[63] not in Heaven or Hell but in the interplay of natural forces (specifically the explosive power of subterranean water and air heated by underground fires).[64] By privileging the scientific origins of the disaster, he places himself within a small, albeit influential, group of Portuguese thinkers who come to represent the cultural aspirations of the Pombaline regime.[65]

Although we have no clear understanding of the political, religious, or scientific motives of the marginalia author, he does appear to counter Moreira de Mendonça by painting a more destructive and dramatic picture of the tragedy. According to him, the Lisbon fire lasted not several days, but more than a month. In the case of the tsunami, he provides more specific details about the damage to the *Terreiro do Paço* than any previous eyewitness. So specific are those details, in fact, that it seems likely that the annotator not only personally inspected the devastated area after the disaster, but recorded those experiences on paper (referring to them several years later when he wrote the marginalia). The earthquake, it appears, made a powerful impression on him. And although he may not have published his own account of the great event, he clearly wished that his recollections of it would be known to posterity. By recording them in a highly readable script inside a copy of Moreira de Mendonça's seminal work, the annotator no doubt believed that they would be preserved well into the future. In this, he has been proven correct.

---

[61] While some scholars accept Moreira de Mendonça's figure of ten thousand victims, others, like Álvaro S. Pereira, argue for much higher numbers, usually between fifteen thousand and forty thousand.

[62] Kendrick, pp. 107–09.

[63] António Nunes Ribeiro Sanches, *Tratado da Conservação da Saude dos Povos* (Lisbon: 1756). Pombal was said to be a strong supporter of Ribeiro Sanches's work, which offered advice on how to improve sanitary conditions in Lisbon after the earthquake. Kendrick, pp. 60–61.

[64] Although Pombal was a vigorous reformer, he was not a *philosophe*. State censors in Portugal banned the works of Rousseau, Spinoza, Locke, Voltaire, Hobbes, and Diderot during his ministry. H. V. Livermore, *A New History of Portugal* (Cambridge: Cambridge University Press, 1966), pp. 236–37.

[65] See Kendrick, pp. 43–71, and Kenneth Maxwell, *Pombal: Paradox of the Enlightenment* (Cambridge: Cambridge University Press, 1995).

One trusts that further study will reveal more about him and his relationship to the events he describes.

I am grateful for the help of Djalma Britto (São Luís, MA, Brazil), George Brown (Seton Hall University), Kirsten Schultz (Seton Hall University), and Michael Inman and the staff at the Rare Books Division of the New York Public Library.

SETON HALL UNIVERSITY, NJ

Abstracts

History Recycled: Contemporary Performances of Shakespeare's 'Richard II' at Portuguese National Theatres
FRANCESCA CLARE RAYNER

ABSTRACT. This article examines claims that contemporary performance has rejected politics by analysing two performances of *Richard II* at Portuguese national theatres. The first, directed by Carlos Avilez at the Teatro Nacional Dona Maria II in Lisbon in 1995, is seen as an example of heritage theatre built upon aesthetic formalism. However, the usual critical association of such performances with political conservatism is challenged. The second, directed by Nuno Cardoso at the Dona Maria and also at Porto's Teatro Carlos Alberto in 2007, is seen as a postmodern form of 'resistant' performance which focuses attention on the politics of male power through ludic parody.
KEYWORDS. Politics, performance, Shakespeare, *Richard II*, Portugal.

RESUMO. O artigo confronta visões correntes sobre a ausência de intervenção política nas encenações teatrais dos anos de 1990 e 2000 através da análise das produções de *Ricardo II* de Shakespeare nos teatros nacionais portugueses. A primeira encenação, dirigida por Carlos Avilez no Teatro Nacional D. Maria II em Lisboa em 1995, é vista como um exemplo de 'heritage theatre' e formalismo estético. Contudo, a usual associação crítica deste tipo de produção com conservadorismo político é contestada pela autora. A segunda produção, dirigida por Nuno Cardoso no Dona Maria e no Teatro Carlos Alberto do Porto em 2007, é vista como uma forma pósmoderna de performance 'resistente', focalizada na paródia ao poder masculino.
PALAVRAS CHAVE. Política, performance, Shakespeare, *Richard II*, Portugal.

Images of Defeat: Early Fado Films and the Estado Novo's Notion of Progress
MICHAEL COLVIN

ABSTRACT. At the turn of the 1930s, the debut of Portugal's first talkies, Leitão de Barros's *A Severa* and Cottinelli Telmo's *A Canção de Lisboa*, coincides with the ideological and cultural reorientation of the Estado Novo, signalled by the inauguration of the *Secretariado da Propaganda Nacional* (SPN). Starting in 1933, the Portuguese government promotes a national cinema that it hopes will project the progress of the Estado Novo as it reflects on the grandeur of previous centuries of Portuguese history. And as *Severa* and *Canção* appear before the establishment of Portugal's ministry of propaganda, these films do not adhere to the SPN's directives for national cinema. As a result, these movies present values and images that, shortly thereafter, will be purged from Portuguese movies for the rest of the decade: values linked to a people who are dissatisfied with the previous quarter of a century of experimental democracy, yet who are cynical about the seemingly progressive ideals of the nascent regime. And as the Fado, bullfights, and folklore are common motifs in *Severa* and *Canção*, these films allow us to observe a dialogue between Portugal's first talkies and to catch a glimpse of the Nation's popular culture before the Estado Novo's propaganda has a chance to recontextualize it to promote its own agenda.

KEYWORDS. Estado Novo, cinema, *A Severa*, Leitão de Barros, *A Canção de Lisboa*, Cottinelli Telmo, fado, propaganda, Ferro.

RESUMO. No início da década de 1930, a estreia dos primeiros filmes sonoros portugueses, *A Severa* de Leitão de Barros e *A Canção de Lisboa* de Cottinelli Telmo, acompanha a reorientação ideológica e cultural do Estado Novo que coincide com a inauguração do *Secretariado da Propaganda Nacional* (SPN). A partir de 1933, o governo português promove um cinema nacional com o fim de propagar o progresso do Estado Novo e também reflectir a grandeza da história portuguesa dos séculos anteriores. Como *Severa* e *Canção* estreiam antes do estabelecimento do SPN, estes filmes não estão sujeitos às directivas da propaganda nacional. Aliás, estes filmes apresentam valores e imagens que brevemente desaparecerão do cinema português até ao fim da década: valores ligados a um povo desencantado com o prévio quartel de um século de democracia experimental e ainda cínico quanto aos aparentes ideais progressivos de um regime novo. E como o fado, a tauromaquia e o folclore constituem motivos partilhados por *Severa* e *Canção*, estes filmes permitem-nos observar um diálogo entre os primeiros filmes sonoros portugueses e espreitarmos assim a cultura popular nacional antes da propaganda estado-novista conseguir recontextualizá-la com o fim de promover a sua própria missão.

PALAVRAS CHAVE. Estado Novo, cinema, *A Severa*, Leitão de Barros, *A Canção de Lisboa*, Cottinelli Telmo, fado, propaganda, Ferro.

The Aquatic Unconscious: Water Imagery in Eça de Queirós's 'A Cidade e as Serras'
ESTELA VIEIRA

ABSTRACT. This essay provides a close reading of the water imagery in Eça de Queirós's late work *A Cidade e as Serras*, reinforcing the complexity of this deceptively simple novel whose multifaceted meanings have too often been oversimplified by criticism. It argues that the symbolic aquatic constellation the author connects to plot and character development functions to create an awareness of depth and ambiguity that replicates Jacinto's unconsciousness, and ironically suggests a Portuguese collective unconscious. Since Portugal's political dominance has depended on the sea, the author's satirical discourse, built around the ubiquitous aquatic metaphors, serves to undermine the country's hegemonic project. Hence far from being retrograde, the novel with its irony and humour generates a significant critique of Portugal's failed expansionist ambitions.

KEYWORDS. Eça de Queirós, *A Cidade e as Serras*, *The City and the Mountains*, novel, water, aquatic, Portugal.

RESUMO. Este ensaio propõe uma leitura aprofundada das imagens aquáticas numa obra do último Eça, *A Cidade e as Serras*, reforçando assim a complexidade deste romance cujos múltiplos significados a crítica durante muito tempo simplificou. Nesta perspectiva, a constelação aquática simbólica que o autor liga ao desenvolvimento das personagens e do enredo funciona para criar um conhecimento de profundidade e ambiguidade que reproduz a inconsciência de Jacinto e sugere uma inconsciência colectiva portuguesa. Já que o domínio político de Portugal sempre dependeu do mar,

o discurso satírico que o autor constrói com as ubíquas metáforas aquáticas serve para censurar o projecto hegemónico do país. Longe de ser retrógrado, com a sua ironia e humor o romance gera uma crítica significativa das falidas ambições expansionistas de Portugal.
PALAVRAS CHAVE. Eça de Queirós, *A Cidade e as Serras*, romance, água, aquático, Portugal.

Zola in Rio de Janeiro: The Production of Space in Aluísio Azevedo's 'O Cortiço'
LÚCIA SÁ

ABSTRACT. This article focuses on spatial relations and practices in Aluísio Azevedo's *O Cortiço* (1890). Critics have been for the most part reluctant to accept that Azevedo was attempting to make clear political claims through his novel. His fate has not been, in this sense, very different from that of his French model, Émile Zola. Marxist criticism has been especially remarkable for its outright rejection of naturalism's negative analyses of capitalism, particularly following Lukács's critique of Zola's 'excessive' use of descriptions in his novel. My contention is that it is precisely because Azevedo assigned a central role to space in his novel (and not in spite of it) that he strengthened his analysis of the profound inequalities inherent in the modernizing of Brazilian society in the aftermath of the Republic. The main lesson Azevedo seems to have learned from his French Master, then (apart, of course, from specific situations and certain similar characters), was the critique of the dominant economic and social order of his time, which is done, in both authors, through a rupture with what Schor called the 'hegemony of the French psychological novel'.
KEYWORDS. *O Cortiço*, *The Slum*, Aluísio Azevedo, space, Marxism, social critique, economic conditions, slavery, capitalism.

RESUMO. O tema deste artigo são as relações e práticas espaciais no romance *O Cortiço* (1890), de Aluísio Azevedo, autor que, para a maioria dos críticos, nunca demonstrou capacidade de análise social profunda em seus romances. A recepção de Aluísio, nesse sentido, não difere muito da de seu modelo, o francês Émile Zola. A crítica marxista, particularmente, tem se caracterizado por uma grande antipatia pelas análises de autores naturalistas sobre o sistema capitalista, especialmente após a publicação dos ensaios de Lukács sobre o 'excesso' de descrições nos romances de Zola. O que pretendo demonstrar neste trabalho é que é precisamente graças à posição central que o espaço ocupa em *O Cortiço*, e não apesar dessa centralidade, que Aluísio logrou, a meu ver, uma análise bastante competente, das profundas desigualdades sociais inerentes ao processo de modernização do Brasil na época da proclamação da República. A principal lição que Aluísio parece ter aprendido do seu mestre francês (além, é claro, de certas situações específicas e personagens semelhantes) foi a crítica da ordem econômica e social do seu tempo, que se faz, em ambos os autores, pela ruptura com o que Schor denominou a 'hegemonia do romance psicológico francês'.
PALAVRAS CHAVE. *O Cortiço*, Aluísio Azevedo, espaço, Marxismo, crítica social, condições econômicas, escravidão, capitalismo.

The Brazil of Sílvio Romero and Machado de Assis: History of a 'Polemic', or the Writer as Critic of the Critic
ALBERTO SCHNEIDER

ABSTRACT. This article explores the political, aesthetic and intellectual divergences between the historian of literature Sílvio Romero and the writer Machado de Assis, who were contemporaries and founding members of the Academia Brasileira de Letras. In 1897 Romero wrote his *Machado de Assis: estudo comparativo de literatura brasileira*, in which he criticizes the writer for his supposed weakness in the discussion of the great national questions — the end of slavery, European immigration, national identity and miscegenation. However, this was an agenda, inspired by social Darwinism, that was rejected by Machado. It is argued here that, contrary to the supposition of many Brazilian critics — for whom Romero had 'not understood' Machado — the historian was able to see very clearly in the man of letters a different interpretation of Brazil, one that directly contested the one that he was advancing.
KEYWORDS. Machado de Assis, Sílvio Romero, positivism, race, Brazil.

RESUMO. Este artigo explora as divergências políticas, estéticas e intelectuais entre o historiador da literatura Sílvio Romero e o escritor Machado de Assis. Ambos foram contemporâneos e membros fundadores da Academia Brasileira de Letras. Em 1897, Romero escreve *Machado de Assis: estudo comparativo de literatura brasileira*, onde critica o escritor por sua suposta tibieza em refletir sobre as grandes questões nacionais — o esgotamento da escravidão, a imigração européia, a identidade nacional, a miscegenação. Machado recusara esta agenda, inspirada no darwinismo social. Ao contrário do que supôs a crítica brasileira — para quem Romero 'não entendera' Machado — o historiador foi capaz de reconhecer no literato outra interpretação do Brasil, em franca oposição àquela na qual ele próprio acreditava.
PALAVRAS CHAVE. Machado de Assis, Sílvio Romero, positivismo, raça, Brasil.

A New Account of the Lisbon Earthquake: Marginalia in Joaquim José Moreira de Mendonça's 'Historia Universal dos Terremotos'
MARK MOLESKY

ABSTRACT. This article will translate and comment upon a previously unknown Portuguese eyewitness account of the 1755 Lisbon Earthquake written in the margins of a New York Public Library copy of Joaquim José Moreira de Mendonça's seminal *Historia Universal dos Terremotos* (1758). Rendered in brown ink and highly legible handwriting consistent with the eighteenth century, these anonymous annotations provide a brief, but valuable, perspective on all three phases of the Lisbon disaster: the earthquake, the tsunami, and the subsequent fire.
KEYWORDS. Lisbon earthquake, tsunami, marginalia, eyewitness.

RESUMO. Este artigo oferece uma tradução e um comentário sobre um testemunho, até hoje desconhecido, do grande terramoto de Lisboa de 1755 que foi escrito nas margens de um exemplar da *Historia Universal dos Terremotos* (1758) de Joaquim José Moreira de Mendonça conservado na New York Public Library. Escrito com uma tinta castanha e numa letra bem legível e datável do século dezoito, estas anotações oferecem uma perspectiva breve, mas valiosa, das três fases do desastre de Lisboa: o terramoto, o tsunami, e o fogo.
PALAVRAS CHAVE. Lisboa, terramoto, tsunami, *marginalia*, testemunha.

www.ingramcontent.com/pod-product-compliance
Lightning Source LLC
Chambersburg PA
CBHW061418300426
44114CB00015B/1984